40 Fulfilled Events Foreshadowing Tribulation.

By
Mary Young

Copyright © 2023 Mary Young
All rights reserved. ISBN: 9781915911421
Printed in the United States of America.

If you think the end spoken of in the Bible is coming, you are right. It is soon. "Though it tarry, it will not tarry."

To our Lord Jesus, who has blessed me and bestowed His grace to undertake this endeavor for people that He loves so much. His love and guidance have been with me my whole life. I hope these pages are a testament to Your goodness, wisdom, and mercy.

May this book serve as a beacon of hope and inspiration to all who read it, and may it bring glory to Your holy name. Thank you, Lord, for Your unending love and for the privilege of sharing Your message with the world. Amen.

I dedicate this book to Lemmy and Tinsai Dida who are prayer warriors, and evangelists in the remote areas of Ethiopia, and who were my second round of confirmers in the gifting (after Heidi Baker and her assistant) in the prophetic from the Lord to me. A prophetic friend of theirs in Ethiopia told them my name, and that they would meet me in the U.S. and my sister befriended them in the local traffic court.

When they heard about me, they said they knew my name ahead of time from their prophetic friend, and that I was the one with the gifting. The Lord has shown me many things I am including in this book to confirm for non-believers and those on the fence that everything the Bible has declared about this time has come true, and there are still yet others to be fulfilled.

This book has been a challenge as it seems every week now there is some new thing happening in the world that means the "birth pangs" Jesus mentioned are coming more frequently and with intensity. New content keeps coming to me, which delays the book's publishing as I add it here. Do not wait for the sweetness of the Lord and His Holy Spirit to live in you. Today is the day of salvation!

As He says in John 9:4, "I must work the works of Him who sent me, while it is day; for the night cometh when no man can work." Jesus is referring to the time when we will no longer share the gospel because the "Fullness of the Gentiles" has happened, and this work will be complete.

I thank my family for their patience, as it was time away from them to complete this. Thank you, my husband, David, daughter Laryn and sister Kathy.

An example of the fullness of the Gentiles: there is Heidi Baker's mission in Mozambique, where they have translated every language there to solar bibles so that everyone in every town has access to read it. Since the Bible says that every "ethnos" (people group) will be reached before the end, then we are close to the time.

Jesus is waiting to live inside you, and He made it simple that you would accept Him so that He can take away your sins and believe that He died and rose again on the third day and that you would believe He is giving His life everlasting! And bonus, He gives you "sozo," which means healing of body, soul, and spirit.

You can think of this as the ABCs of salvation:

Admit that you are a sinner in need of a savior. Romans 3:23 "For all have sinned and fallen short of the glory of God and all are justified freely by His grace through the redemption that came by Christ Jesus."

Believe that He died and was gone for two days and on the third day He rose from the dead. 1 Corinthians 15:3 "He was buried, He was raised on the third day according to the Scriptures and that He appeared to Cephas and then to the twelve. After that He appeared to more than 500 brethren."

Commit to a relationship with Jesus, ask Him into your heart and to forgive your sins. The Holy Spirit will indwell inside of you! "For God so loved the world that He gave His only begotten Son that whoever believes in Him shall not perish, but have eternal life."

Get baptized! Mark 16:16 "Whoever believes and is baptized will be saved, but whoever does not believe will be condemned." Please get planted in a full Bible believing church as if you did all of this you are now and forever part of the body of Christ of which He is the head and you will come with us (His bride the church) in the rapture!

I write this because I love you, friend, and I would want no one to make the wrong decision and end up in hell. It is real; it was made for fallen angels, but as Jesus says, it is a place of wailing and gnashing of teeth. He refers to Hades 9 times and Gehenna 12 times and both are considered references to hell.

I am going to keep this book deliberately short, as I want the content to be compelling, and for those that do not like to read volumes, God wants to reach the unsaved! The point is to show the amazing truth that the scriptures foretold everything that is happening right now! Come and see for yourself.

We are given a brief time here to get things right. Everyone knows they have sinned, and I know this is true as scripture even says, "No man is righteous, no not one," except for Jesus, who is fully God and human. For any that are long-time Christians, great! But do not think that you are saved just because your parents or grandparents were saved.

Everyone must make their confession before the Lord and invite Him in. As He states about the vine and the branches, those that are not fruitful (abiding in Him) will be gathered up and thrown into the fire. Jesus mentions hell as He gives warning to everyone because He wants all to receive His saving grace.

Table of Contents

INTRODUCTION — 10
CHAPTER 1 THE DECEIVERS — 11
  EVENT #1 DECEIVERS — 11
CHAPTER 2 PHYSICAL EVENTS — 14
  EVENT #2 WARS — 14
  EVENT #3 BUNKERS — 15
  EVENT #4 EARTHQUAKES & VOLCANOES — 16
  EVENT #5 FAMINE — 17
  EVENT #6 PESTILENCE — 18
  EVENT #7 FIRES — 23
  EVENT #8 HAILSTORMS — 24
  EVENT #9 FLOODING — 25
  EVENT #10 DROUGHT — 26
  EVENT #11 RIVERS DRY UP — 27
  EVENT #12 SIGNS THE EARTH IS DYING — 28
  EVENT #13 LOCUSTS — 29
CHAPTER 3 SIGNS CONCERNING ISRAEL — 30
  EVENT #14 ISRAEL RETURNS — 30
  EVENT #15 RED HEIFERS — 33
  EVENT #16 ISRAEL'S HIGH-SPEED TRAIN — 34
  EVENT #17 THE GREAT DIASPORA — 34
  EVENT #18 ISRAELI WAR 1967 — 35
  EVENT #19 ISRAEL PROSPERS — 36
  EVENT #20 THE GANG UP OF THE WORLD — 36

Chapter 4 SIGNS FOR A ONE WORLD GOVERNMENT — 37
Event #21 Climate Commandments — 37
Event #22 One World Religion — 40
Event #23 Technology in the Bible — 41
Event #24 CBDC — 42

Chapter 5 EVIL IN THE LAST DAYS — 45
Event #25 Knowledge Shall Increase — 45
Event #26 Level of Evil — 46
Event #27 Lawlessness — 49
Event #28 Anti-Christ is Here — 49
Event #29 Zeitgeist — 50
Event #30 Satan's Earth System — 51
Event #31 Mockers and Scoffers — 52
Event #32 Family Turns Against Each Other — 53

Chapter 6 ESCHATOLOGY — 54
Event #33 World Timeline — 54
Event #34 Blood Moon Tetrads — 55
Event #35 When Jesus Returns — 56
Event #36 Global Leaders — 57
Event #37 Peace and Safety — 59

Chapter 7 FUTURE EVENTS - A "NOW" WORD — 60
Event #38 Tribulation Soon — 60
Event #39 Rapture Time — 62
Event #40 Four Horses — 64

Post Log — 68
Bibliography — 70
About the Author — 73

God's creation speaks for Him. Even the rocks will cry out.

INTRODUCTION

The Lord put this book in my spirit back around Christmas of 2021. I work with the homeless right in my backyard to address their needs and share the Lord, who turns everything into wonder and goodness. I wanted to continue to serve them, but He wanted me to also write a short book so that He could reach others who are questioning what is happening right now worldwide.

It is always important to test the spirits and hone your ability to know that it is God giving you the instruction, but the cool thing is for me; He always gives me confirmation of things and I will share some instances in this book of these. He would tell me something happening now, and I researched after and found it to be a strong and true word.

Accurate prophecy is all in the Bible. The Lord has many passages where something happened again later that He foretold. Also, some of these prophecies are happening again here at the end. The same devastations the Lord used to shake up the sleepy and call them to Himself are reoccurring. Ecclesiastes 3:15. "What is happening now has happened before, and what will happen in the future has happened before, because God makes the same things happen over and over again." All the plagues the Egyptians had to get the Jews out of Egypt are happening again.

An example of a prophetic event is rivers turning completely red, like the Dead Sea. This turned red in 2023 at the feast of Atonement. God does things at His "moedim" or special appointed times.

Chapter 1
The Deceivers

Event #1

Don't be deceived! The Lord explains that many will come in the last few days claiming to be Him. A key to survival in these end times is not being deceived. We can know that this is true by looking at people who have claimed to be Him. One such man is Sergei Torop. He is a former police officer who claims to be the reincarnation of Jesus. (Nowhere in the Bible does it say He will be reincarnated as Jesus has been alive after the 3rd day when he was resurrected.) John Miller, (known as A.J.) makes the same claim that he is the reincarnation of Jesus and that his wife is the reincarnation of Mary Magdalene. This is blasphemy as Jesus will marry His bride, the church, when the time is right. They also call their cult "Divine Truth", but Jesus says He is the way, the truth, and the life. Biblically speaking, Jesus does not return until he comes for the awesome and terrible day of the Lord, when He comes to divide the goats from the sheep.

A key to not being deceived is knowing what is in God's word! David Shayler, who is a former MI5 officer and whistle-blower who, in the summer of 2007, proclaimed himself to be the Messiah. He has produced a series of YouTube videos stating this claim. Maurice Clemmons, an American felon responsible for the 2009 murder of 4 police officers in my state of Washington, referred to himself as Jesus.

Todd Kincannon, former head of the South Carolina Republican Party, 2018, mutilated his mother's dog, claiming to police that he was the second coming of Jesus Christ, and that God told him to do this.

Cabbie Hannah, an American internet personality and songwriter, did a rant on TikTok in August 2022 claiming to be the second coming of Christ. All of this, while interesting, there is another possibility of how deception can be construed. Many pastors are teaching false things about who Jesus is. They portray him almost as a genie in a bottle that can fulfill whatever you can think of. The list of these is almost too big to be exhaustive here, and I don't wish to call them out. It saddens me to see many people attending these churches and being fooled into a cheapened Jesus who makes it all about "you" when really it is all about Him and who He is, and how He wants to create a relationship with you that will be everlasting, and so full of the fruit of the Spirit. As Galatians 5:22 states; "But the fruit of the Spirit is love, joy, peace, long-suffering, gentleness, goodness, faith, meekness, and self-control against such things there is no law. And they that are Christ's have crucified the flesh with the affections and lusts. If we live in the Spirit, let us also walk in the Spirit. Let us not be desirous of vain glory, provoking one another, and envying one another."

Do not put over-emphasis each week on how God can fulfill your every dream. We are told first most, to take up our cross and follow Him. What would it say to those who are martyrs in other countries to see a cheapened Jesus? That is not who they are giving their lives for.

The Jews have a very special Rabbi that they claim is rare and that comes along only after many generations. He has memorized the Tanakh, which comprises the Torah, the prophets Nevi'im, and the writings Ketuvim. This would be nigh unto impossible for me or anyone else. He is also attributed to having done several major miracles, and he has a special title of "Yanuka". The most prominent Rabbis in Jerusalem have not only accepted him but claimed him to be their messiah and they have also announced they will soon "reveal" the messiah and you can be sure this is the guy. They also say he is a genius. His title is "Yanuka" but his actual name is "Rav Shlomo Yehuda Ben David". Although he has not claimed to be the Messiah himself, he is certainly letting others make claims without correction.

If he is walking around here now, he is not Jesus as Jesus will be in the air for the rapture, and after that, he will come back with us His church, His army in the sky, on the great and terrible day of the Lord: Commonly known as judgment day. The only supernatural beings to come onto the scene near the same time as the rapture, will be the false prophet, the AntiChrist, and the beast.

Anything that people are doing in the church that goes against God and that is done deliberately with no remorse or desire to correct is antichrist. In this last time, you can see things in church that you did not see twenty years ago.

Chapter 2
Physical Events

This chapter is about physical events on the earth that are all global in nature. In 2000, 2010, and 2020, many conjectured that the tribulation would start. They did not know their Bibles well enough. What the Bible says to look for are disasters that are <u>global</u> events, and not restricted to one area or one country. We have arrived right at the cusp.

Event #2

Wars and rumors of war. We had World War I, World War 2, and many are calling this Ukraine and Russia war World War 3. This has been going on for a long time.

The current war between Ukraine (U.S. for resources and money shipped out) and Russia is really WWIII. We have also seen the largest war games ever run after the Chinese balloon incident over U.S. soil.

What comes before the tribulation is given by Jesus in Matthew 24:3 His disciples ask Him, "Tell us when shall these things be? And what shall be the sign of the coming (2nd coming) and the end of the world? (Also known as the Day of the Lord)" Jesus answers, "Take heed that no man deceives you." (Implies that there will be people doing deception.) "For many shall come in my name saying I am the Christ; and shall deceive many. And ye shall hear of wars and rumors of wars; see that you are not troubled; for all these things must come to pass, but the end is not yet. For nation (ethnos) will rise against nation and kingdom against kingdom; and there shall be famines, pestilences, and earthquakes in diverse places. All these are the beginning of sorrows. Then shall they deliver you up to be afflicted, and shall kill you, and you shall be hated of all nations for My name's sake. And then shall many be offended and shall betray one another and shall hate one another. And many false prophets shall rise and shall deceive many. And because iniquity shall abound, the love of many shall wax cold. But he that shall endure unto the end, the same shall be saved. And this gospel of the kingdom shall be preached in all the world for a witness unto all nations (ethnos or ethnicities), and then the end shall come."

Luke 20 "And when you see Jerusalem compassed about, know that the desolation thereof is nigh." Right now, Israel is in turmoil because the minority far left is fighting against the right, and it is so close to civil war. Even the military and judges are in dissension.

Hot off the presses as of 2/3/2023 the "START" treaty even endured the cold war, is now up for signing and Putin has decided not to sign it. "START" was the reason that we had some peace of mind because both sides would know anytime nuclear weapons were moved anywhere (all the locations of said missiles). A perfect example was the Cuban missile crisis. Recent pictures this week of missiles being moved somewhere as pictures came up of Russia moving them. This combined with a Russian war minister going to Caracas, Venezuela to discuss the safe storage of missiles there is destabilizing, as so close to the U.S.

This next is a good segment with a lot of the end time prophetic from our savior Himself, in His words. The hard part as a Christian is girding myself with the full armor of God so that I can withstand the persecution for Christians that is mentioned in the prior passage of scripture. Yikes! That is okay, and I have prayed a lot, having lived in a cushy country with all the amenities it provides. We need to toughen up and maintain our posture of love to get through all of this.

Event #3

Bunkers, but not for everyone. Elites are the ones that have them all over the world. There are many bunkers In Switzerland. These things can cost millions and in Switzerland alone there are 374,142 bunkers, according to Johnny Harris, who spent some months there investigating and searching these out in the mountains using drones for better visibility as some of these are camouflaged.

It makes sense that the Swiss would have these given that they are the largest money laundering and storage for the wealthy of colossal sums of money. When you don't want your money tracked, this is the place to be. Interesting that the rich don't want you and me having money that is unaccounted for, don't you think? Most of these bunkers are in the mountains, but there are also quite a number that are under peoples' houses. That seems very practical, as for most when things go south, would already be in their home.

Famous people like Elon Musk, and Bill Gates, are not the only ones giving the thumbs up to bunkers, it is also doctors, architects, and lawyers among many professions that have the money to start in at the ground floor of a bunker system. Many of these folks already have enough land where their house is arranged to do something on their properties. One bunker company called Rising S Bunkers out of Texas said that there are 2000% more inquiries from possible buyers worried about their futures. Isaiah 2:10-12 "When the Lord comes to shake the earth, people will hide in holes and caves in the rocky hills to try to escape from His anger and to hide from His powered glory!" A day is coming when human pride will be ended and human arrogance destroyed. Then the Lord will be exalted. On that day, the Lord Almighty will humble everyone powerful, everyone who is proud and conceited."

I imagine that people in Jesus' time wouldn't understand "bunkers" but would understand holes and caves.

Event #4

Earthquakes in diverse places. Please look at the USGS website, and you can see the huge uptick in earthquakes and volcanoes. These have been worldwide for the past 5 years, more than before 2017.

We are seeing an order of magnitude of earthquakes with increasing intensity, and in diverse places that had been quiet for a long time. In addition, the level of volcanic activity has surged around the world. A notable example of earthquakes is happening right now in Turkey and Assyria, where over 50,000 at last count have died. This is a substantial number. The interesting thing is that this earthquake zone is over 500 miles wide and continues to be active currently with sizable quakes continuing as of this writing. Tsunamis have resulted and have been more common in the past 15 years. Luke 21:25 "There will be signs in the sun and moon and stars, and on the earth dismay among the nations, perplexed by the roaring of the sea and the surging of the waves."

Event #5

Famine is now worldwide. This has even come to us in the U.S. where millions do not have enough to eat, and the amount of homeless is off the charts.

In any area of the U.S., you can see huge tent cities. In California, Skid Row has drifted west from Los Angeles Street toward the Loft District, butting up against Main Street, and south in the fashion and flower districts. Estimates of this population are in the tens of thousands.

In Washington State where I live, on any day you can see tents along 99 and in Lynnwood and Everett, there are multiple locations in each. There are 4 to 5 year waiting lists for any housing, and not enough is planned to go up soon. Seattle has more plans for housing, but their problems for homelessness are exponentially greater.

Famine has also been a planned event. What I mean by that is Ukraine is the largest for wheat production and all those fields are decimated. China has 1/3 of all wheat stored, whether they are doing it to protect their supply, or because they don't want the West to have it, it doesn't matter as the outcome is the same. This situation has been devastating to those countries in Africa that mostly depended on these two sources. What is less obvious is the destruction and buyout of farmland happening around our country, the Netherlands, Australia, and others. All of this is conveniently left out of the mainstream corporate news. There are only five large corporations that own all our mainstream media. They can label people investigating "conspiracy theorists" because they have given only one side of a story. Back in the days of Huntley Brinkley's news hour, they always gave two or more sides to a story. Since when is there only one avenue that can be given? Since Nazi Germany when this happened before.

Why have food processing plants and storage facilities having to do with grains mysteriously burned down? For 2022, there were twice as many fires for these facilities as in 2021. The other head-scratcher is that when you read about these individuals for their local news, they all have fire departments that went out to investigate, but they almost only have reports that the "cause is unknown" and there never seems to be a follow-up that gives any real good reason. There were two in Texas, both in early October 2022. One was an Amazon distribution plant, and the other was a Walmart distribution center. Guess we didn't need these?

It is hard not to use the words "planned famine" as mainstream media like CNN tell us that there will be shortages. They know that Ukraine and Russia have bombed and ruined land and resources that would be exported. China has been stock-piling wheat, maybe because they remember a time in the 60s when they had not planned well, and millions died. Farmers in the Netherlands and Australia have had their government shut down their operations, and for some, they were generational farms. They have shut down cow and chicken farms. Want a good bug sandwich? You can see a commercial on the World Economic Forum website with a Hollywood star eating a bug sandwich (as some meat substitute) and acting like it is good tasting.

This is falling into place for Revelation 6:6 "And I heard a voice amid the four beasts saying, "A measure of wheat for a penny, and three measures of barley for a penny; and see thou not hurt the oil and wine." A penny is worth much more back in the day of John the Revelator. This passage is about famine and the cost of food worldwide. You would have to work all day to afford bread, as he shared.

Event #6

Global pestilence and, for the first time, the World Health Organization ran the entire world telling it what it had to do for response and procedures. This was COVID-19, which was the first ever global lockdown of the world's population, a wonderful experiment to see if the global population could be fear controlled, and maybe even turn them into villainizers of those who would not take the shot.

For the first time, natural immunity was thrown under the bus, along with any naturopathic remedies that were good. Doctor Peter A. McCullough was vice-chief of internal medicine at Baylor University. He is labeled now online as a misinformation promoter, let alone that he had a top level of patients for whom he had an early treatment regimen that worked, and his track record is stellar. Consider that doctors across the country were having the CDC, tell them not to do what they knew worked. They were saying not to administer Vitamin C, or Vitamin D. These are highly effective immune builders until they were called ineffective; As was natural immunity, which has always existed for long-term antibodies for those people who already had the disease and got over it.

You can watch Doctor John Campbell and Doctor Drew Pinsky who have been researching what is effective and why the government pushed only the jabs. This happens when the CDC has a director who has sat on the board of Pfizer, and when media has been paid off by Pfizer, Johnson and Johnson, and other large pharmaceutical companies. Millions are spent on only one answer for the public. It is still true the adage to "follow the money" and it seems we have reached the point where profits are looked at globally for everything. These same folks that pay off our government officials, and pay off CDC and FDA, have also paid off the media in the millions each year. What is the largest media campaign ever run? It is the campaign to make everyone take the jab. Some states even paid their citizens to get them. When Bill Gates pays millions for positive media coverage that is solely targeted at you thinking he is the good guy, well, whoa Nelly, something stinks!

On KTLA 5, a news station for Los Angeles County. USC scientist and professor Adam Smith tested water at waste treatment plants for their out-takes. He did this in two locations, Playa Del Rey and Carson. At both spots, his test results found superbugs living in the water. He stated that Colistin is the strongest antibiotic we must use to treat such things and it does not work against the bugs that he found. Adam says don't overprescribe antibiotics as these superbugs are the result and they are getting stronger. The professor believes we should test at all treatment plants regularly. Right! Chris Wolf was the reporter on this video from KTLA 5.

After Bill Gates sold off most of his Pfizer stock, then he felt he could share that they had underestimated the strength of natural immunity in preventing future outbreaks for individuals who had already contracted the disease and healed of it. Yes, I am personal proof that this is true. Since the original contraction of Omicron, my husband came down with Covid-19, but my daughter and I, who did not take the jab, did not contract it, even though the media said how easily it can spread. Though I am a microcosm of world experience, when talking with friends and family for which I am probably average for my level of contact, everyone knew someone who had the shot and died, but no one among my peers knew anyone who died from the disease itself. I'm not saying that this will hold for everyone but find it in line with statistics shared by Dr. John Campbell who, since the beginning of the pandemic, has tracked all world statistics about it. Since our government did not want to share any information (even labeling any dissenters as misinformation) Dr. John Campbell had to share statistics from other countries who were studying it. It turned out natural immunity was slightly higher in avoiding getting the disease by 2 to 3 percentage points. Plus, as is true for any medications, there are actual side effects that can be detrimental, as in myocarditis and pericarditis from Pfizer in particular, which was included in a judicially required release of information that Pfizer had to share some months back in 2022.

Curiously, when there was a SARS outbreak in 2008 there was found in the wet market what animal it had come from. (Animal zero) and after this, there was another in 2013 that again an animal was located, which was the start of the spread. Covid-19 started back at the end of 2019 and here we are in 2023 with 80,000 animals tested and no animal zero located. In the other outbreaks, the animal was identified within 4 to 6 months.

Sheri Marksman is a journalist and author. She hosts Sky News Australia and wrote a book called "What Happened in Wuhan: A Virus Like No Other". She has unveiled information about the Wuhan leak. The NIH (along with Dr. Fauci) did and still do fund gain of function research in China, no matter how hard he still tries to lie about this. It did escape a lab, as the evidence is the first casualties that died in a nearby hospital of the disease, and they were lab workers from this Chinese lab. The facts are now coming out, and you can watch current senate hearings where they try to get Fauci to admit the truth, and they even have a chain of document letters where he tried to cover the matter up from the very beginning.

Anyone can look up government information on Fauci. Turns out he was given a job at the Department of Defense in bioweapon research (hmm). He has an NIAID budget and a budget from the Department of Defense. Seems thou protesteth much (and frequently) Dr. Fauci! He is the highest-paid government employee making more than the president.

Robert F. Kennedy Jr. has been defending families who have been financially destroyed by pharmaceutical companies pushing vaccines at a young age for our children. He has written a book called "The Real Anthony Fauci, Bill Gates, Big Pharma and the Global War on Democracy and Public Health." His organization is called "Children's Health Defense." I wish I had known what I know now. I would have waited some years before giving my only baby girl shots the week she was born. She was breastfed and had fantastic immunity, so much so that she would get a cold and throw up a bunch of mucus and that was it. She was well within a day. Never seriously ill except for once.

After I had a light case of Covid in 2020, I received a call from someone who was asking me all kinds of invasive questions. I should have just hung up as they were medical, and I thought at first that this was a call from my doctor's office. Once I was fully awake, I said, "Who is this calling?" They said they were from the County Health Department in my county. So, I said, well this is pretty much illegal as HIPPA law says you aren't to collect this information about me so I'm not going to talk about this, so we stopped our conversation at that point. I kick myself for opening up to her out of habit.

Pharmaceutical profits are at their highest level since their inception. And they plan to increase future vaccines per their CEO, to $110 - $130 per dose. Don't think they stopped any plans just because senators are asking questions about vaccine injury. Recently, the NIAID and NIH paid Boston University to combine the Omicron spike with the original Wuhan strain. With humanized mice, there is an 80% kill rate. What is the goal here? Is it only to create something for which the public will need vaccination for profits, or does it also have anything to do with Bill Gates' talks back in 2016/2017 about the overpopulation of the planet?

One might think they could kill two birds with one stone. Speaking of birds, why suddenly are millions of our poultry sick and dying from bird flu? Hint: go look up on the World Economic Forum website for their "facts" around bug meat being more carbon-friendly to the planet. Boy, you can't even make this stuff up!

In the UK, there was a governmental investigation and the CEO of Pfizer Albert Bourla did not attend. His head of development when answering a question blundered and said, "No, we did not have time to do transmission testing, we had to move at the speed of science. We had to understand what was going on in the market and we had to put everything at risk." Translation: we had your governments lie and say that the shot would stop transmission, and we had to make sure our profits were secure by getting a jump on shots being distributed.

There is now a new document that just came out from W.H.O. that tries to place them at the top of international countries, supposedly that they are the experts and that some countries were better than others at handling the pandemic and that there needs to be unanimity letting them handle it. This document also outlines how the distribution of emergency stuff would be through them. Amendments by the Biden administration would circumvent our government, giving it jurisdiction outside of the U.S. to the W.H.O. I found online that when I Googled to get this information, I could not. I had to go to WION (East India News) to find this, as Google immediately uses their filters to state this as misinformation.

Michelle Bachmann, former US Representative, was the only one to attend the meeting in Belgium recently for the W.H.O. No other Senator or Representative from our government attended this important meeting where things are being decided that would supersede our government in the next pandemic. Now the U.K. is already participating in giving over governmental powers to the W.H.O. for anything they deem as a pandemic, and the powers not only include lockdowns, masks and mandating of mRNA based medicines, but also distribution of food and other items of necessity.

Increasingly, we have only one story to listen to, and that is the story of the U.S. government. On February 7th, 2023, Marburg disease (a hemorrhagic fever) was discovered in Equatorial Guinea. The Ministry of Health has reported eight deaths. They have turned over management to the World Health Organization, which set up contact tracing. Thirty-four contacts are currently under follow-up.

However, this does not seem to be the super spreader. What we need to look at is the model of what happened in the past. We had "event 201," where representatives of our global governments ran a simulation of how Covid would be as a pandemic and adjusted as the week of simulation went on; including weeks of lockdowns, media coverage to control the narrative, mandating of masks, incentivizing mRNA shot taking, and nullifying any other drugs or herbs that work. Fast-forward to 2023 and they all did it again at a meeting in Belgium where they did another simulation for a disease they are calling "Seers," which stands for severe, endemic enterovirus, respiratory, syndrome 2025. Apparently, in the simulation, they did the same format from the prior exercise. Everyone gets together and plans for when it will be here, what it will be, and how to control the public, and even runs a simulation of a broadcast where the moderator is a newscaster sharing this scary new virus that will quickly kill children if the vaccinations are not taken, and that there are already 500 deaths. And they have a location for this, wait for it... Brazil. Don't plan a vacation to Brazil in 2025. Revelation 18: 23 "And the light of a candle shall shine no more at all in thee, and the voice of the bridegroom and the bride shall be heard no more at all in thee: for thy merchants were the great men of the earth; for by thy pharmakeia (having to do with pharmaceuticals) were all nations deceived. And in her was found the blood of prophets, and of saints, and of all that were slain upon the earth." Psalm 91: "He that dwelleth in the secret place of the highest shall abide under the shadow of the Almighty. I will say of the Lord, He is my refuge and my fortress; my God, in Him will I trust. Surely He shall deliver thee from the snare of the fowler, and the noise-some pestilence. He shall cover thee with His feathers, and under His wings shalt thou trust; His truth shall be thy shield and buckler. Thou shalt not be afraid for the terror by night, nor for the arrow that flies by day. Nor the pestilence that walketh in darkness; nor the destruction that wasteth at noonday. A thousand may fall at thy side, and ten thousand at thy right hand; but it shall not come nigh thee. Only with thine eyes shalt thou behold and see the reward of the wicked. Because thou hast made the Lord, which is my refuge, even the highest, thy habitation." I believe this with all I am.

Event #7

Fire as never before. I have lived in Washington State my whole life, and we have never had fires so large with thousands of acres of land under flames, as we have had the last five years. So much so that the smoke has "billowed" over to western Washington from eastern Washington. We have had days when the smog was considered too dangerous to breathe in. Joel 2: 30 "I will show wonders in the heavens and on earth, blood and fire and billows of smoke": There are fires that are orders of magnitude larger and with more intensity, than have ever been before in Washington State, Oregon, California, Spain, Australia, Finland (where fires were rare), British Columbia, Siberia, Greece, Turkey, Italy, and Lebanon. Time magazine has a good article on this. For the blood, an example would be the dead sea has turned red as has a canal in Nootdorp Netherlands, Bondi Beach in Australia; the Beirut River in Lebanon, a river in Zhejiang Province, China, and red rain fell in Sevanagala Sri Lanka. Fire has devastated over 2,000,000 acres of land across the globe. Fire season, as a result, has run through the summer and well into winter for us in Washington State. And for the first time, there are fires on the Western side of the state as things continue to be dry. Also, we now see a fire season that goes ten months instead of three or four, as in the past.

Event #8

Hailstones! The Lord sent hailstones after the enemies of Israel in Joshua 10:11 "As they fled from before Israel, while they were at the descent of Beth-Horon, the Lord threw large stones (hailstones) from heaven on them as far as Azekah and they died; there were more who died from hail storms than those whom the sons of Israel killed with the sword." Let me assure you that often in the Bible there is a foreshadowing of coming events. He has often had prophets play out an event for some length of time that they had to endure, to show them what He would bring on a larger scale. Here is an excerpt from Ezekiel 13:11-13 "So tell those who plaster it over with whitewash, that it will fall. A flooding rain will come, and you, o hailstones, will fall; and a violent wind will break out. Behold, when the wall has fallen, will you not be asked, "Where is the plaster with which you plastered it?" Therefore, thus says the Lord GOD, "I will make a violent wind break out in My wrath. There will also be in My anger a flooding rain and hailstones to consume it in my wrath." Job 38:22-23 "Have you entered the storehouses of the snow, or have you seen the storehouses of the hail; Which I have reserved for the time of distress (tribulation reference), for the day of war and battle?"

Psalm 105:32 "He gave them hail for rain, and flaming fire in their land." Haggai 2:17 "I smote you and every work of your hands (for idolatry) with blasting wind mildew and hail, yet you did not come back to Me declares the Lord." The Two Preachers have lots of videos where each week for some years they have been cataloging disasters having to do with flooding and hailstorms. God is increasing His scope, and just to let you know, He is bringing it to places that never saw this type of hyper-hailstorm before. For many, this devastating hail is the size of oranges and penetrates house roofs and car windshields. Places you can look up for yourselves like Villa Paz Argentina. Chunks of hail fell, the largest being 7.4 inches across. Vivian South Dakota has experienced very large hail in the thunderstorms they have had in the last few years. These last signs are global, so other places include Tripoli Libya, Ponca City Oklahoma, Sanandrei Western Romania, Undigen South Western Germany, Slovenia, Aurora, Nebraska, Gopalganj District Bangladesh, Strasbourg

France, Stephenville Texas, Mackay Queensland Australia, and very rare in Badr City Saudi Arabia.

Revelation 16:21 "Hailstones from the sky, huge hailstones each weighing about a hundred pounds fell on people and they cursed God on account of the plague of hail, because the plague was so terrible." It is fascinating. What do you think about people who know for sure that God Himself is doing this thing, yet they want to curse Him?

Event #9

Flooding looking as in the days of Noah! Ezekiel 13:11-13 "Say unto them which daub it with untempered mortar, that it shall fall; there shall be an overflowing shower; and ye, O great hailstones, shall fall; and a stormy wind shall rend it. Lo, when the wall is fallen, shall it not be said unto you, where is the daubing wherewith ye have daubed it?" Matthew 24: 37-39 "But as the days of Noah were, so shall also the coming of the Son of man be (Jesus)." For as in the days that were before the flood, they were eating and drinking, marrying and giving in marriage, until the day that Noah entered the ark, and knew not until the flood came and took them all away; so shall also the coming of the son of man be. The incredible moment a river is reborn in the Israel desert on March 19th, 2014. To the delight of watching locals, a river returned; the waters of the river Zin are gushing down a dry riverbed. For centuries, the area has been dry. The rebirth of a river, after years of drought, has been captured on camera in the Negev desert, Israel. Rivers in the desert! You can find this on YouTube when searching for "Fountains in the Negev." This is also happening in Saudi Arabia and that is on the Channel Eyes 200M. Isaiah 41:18 "I will open rivers in high places, and fountains amid the valleys! I will make the wilderness a pool of water and the dry land springs of water." There has been and is continual severe coastal flooding along the Eastern Seaboard and in Louisiana, Texas, and Florida.

Globally we should include heavily flooded places like Columbia, Venezuela, Mexico, Nicaragua, Trinidad, Puerto Rico, Costa Rica, Java, Sulawesi Islands in Indonesia, Philippines, Sri Lanka, Vietnam, Cambodia, India, Thailand, Pakistan, Japan, Nepal, China, Italy, Crete Greece, Saudi Arabia, Morocco, Maputo, Mozambique, Chad, Nigeria, South Sudan, Ghana, Central African Republic, Cameroon, Mali, Niger, Guinea, South Africa, Uganda, Germany, Belgium, Romania, Bulgaria, France, UK, Spain, Czech

Republic, Croatia, Luxembourg, Netherlands, Switzerland, Bosnia, and Herzegovina.

These are the hardest hits in the last 5 years. For further information please check out https://apnews.com/hub/floods and www.theguardian.com.

Event #10

Drought. Psalm 107:33-34 "He changes rivers into a wilderness and springs of water into a thirsty ground; A fruitful land into a salt waste, because of the wickedness of those who dwell in it." Jeremiah 50:38 "A drought on her waters, and they will be dried up. For it is a land of idols (Do you think there are any idols in our great country?) And they are mad over fearsome idols." Ezekiel 22:23-24 "And the word of the Lord came to me saying, "Son of man, say to her, "You are a land that is not cleansed or rained on in the day of indignation." Leviticus 26: 3-4 "If you walk in My statutes and keep My commandments to carry them out, then I shall give you rains in their season so that the land will yield her increase, and the trees of the field will bear their fruit."

There is a U.S. drought monitor at https://www.drought.gov. You can also check out SPEI Global Drought Monitor, which offers near real-time information about drought conditions at the global scale. Droughts are getting worse, and not just anecdotally. The UN says drought frequency and duration have increased by a third globally since 2000. There is a correlation between places of over-flooding and land that is next to where drought has taken over. CNBC says that climate change is speeding up and desertification is happening in several parts of the earth where there is limited access to water. Of note, I can recall a time when I was looking at investing for the future and my thought was companies that have pure water sources. I was thinking the same as George W. Bush, who has such holdings. Ukraine, which was providing up to a third of wheat and barley, has been affected by drought, and now with the war continuing for 1 year so far, they have fields that will not be used for quite some time. There are so many countries affected I had to consult a drought map: Russia, China, Ukraine, India, much of Europe, Mexico, most of South America, Bangladesh, and the eastern side of Africa, according to Aqueduct by World Resources Institute. An excellent study would be to look up online how the drought worldwide has affected our food supply. With Ukraine and China they have limited exports, which has caused starvation for many African countries that have relied upon them in the past. Scientists say that Europe may face the worst drought in 500 years, the Guardian reports!

Event #11

Rivers drying up? The Lord directed me to how big the Euphrates river was; that much is said of it in the Bible. It caught my eye, an important river that supported people through multiple nations. When news of this large one drying up came to my attention as it had dwindled to almost empty and it used to be huge, I felt sadness. The Lord told me to go look up all the major rivers of the world because the end times are global. Levels are at extreme lows in all the major river systems, which surprised me. The Colorado River, Volga, Rhine, Danube, Yangtze, Tiber, Po, Elbe, Euphrates, and Tigris. Of special note is the Nile River, as it is under assault on two fronts. 1) A massive dam upstream in Ethiopia and 2) Rising sea levels leading to saltwater intrusion downstream. (Published by Yale Environmental 360.) The Lord has a lot to say about the Euphrates River. Isaiah 11:15 "The Lord will dry up the gulf of the Egyptian sea; with a scorching wind, he will sweep His hand over the Euphrates River. He will break it up into seven streams so that anyone can cross over in sandals." Isaiah 19:5 "The waters of the river will dry up, and the riverbed will be parched and dry. The canals will stink; the streams of Egypt will dwindle and dry up. The reeds and rushes will wither, also the plants along the Nile, at the mouth of the river. Every sown field along the Nile will become parched, will blow away, and be no more."

So, who is buying up the water in the big water grab for the future? Smart investors, for sure; Goldman Sachs, JP Morgan, Chase, Citigroup, UBS, Deutsche Bank Credit Suisse, Barclays Bank, The Blackstone Group, Allianz, HSBC Bank, also wealthy tycoons like T. Bone Pickens, George W Bush, Hong Kong's Li Lashing, Philippine's Marvel V Panginan to mention the largest. They are all buying thousands of acres of land with aquifers, lakes, waters, water utilities, and shares in water engineering. Want to play a good game of Monopoly?

Event #12

Your earth is dying. I know, I know, all the New Agers are thinking there is about to be a great regeneration, but the great regeneration will be that the Lord says He will create a new heaven and a new earth. Can't wait! When Adam and Eve sinned, evil entered the world, and the world gradually has been in decay ever since. It is not just pollution. No, this is groaning for the Lord to make things new again. Romans 8:22 "For we know that the whole creation groans and travails in pain together until now." Nature suffers with us because we have fallen. But God the Father has a plan to make this all corrected. He gave us this so that we could be redeemed through Jesus first. Then there will be His creation of a new earth and new heavens.

It is important to note that climate change is being dealt with in a dangerous way to the planet. In an attempt to do cooling, for some time now there has been "seeding" in the skies by planes that are designed to be able to successfully eject materials that reflect back the sun to help cool the earth. In theory that might sound good, but you should definitely check out Dane Wigington's website www.geoengineeringwatch.org for information on the effects this could have on our planet. They have done in their lab, studies of what are the particulates being released. They are releasing nanoparticles of graphene, silica, aluminum oxide, titanium oxide and others. The U.S. holds patents for airplanes that are designed to release and seed. Alan Buckmann, a U.S. Air Force man, has verified that they are leaving chemtrails that only these specialized jets can do. Commercial jets are designed to be very clean and do not leave the big trails in the sky. Catherine Austin Fitts, a government employee, verified that this is in fact happening. Christine Trame PHD says the particles are radioactive and toxic to human bodies and to animal life.

Dane's team has gone up high in the atmosphere to collect samples right after a spraying from the contrail of one of these planes. They found all of these specific trace nano-particles when analyzing the samples. There are films where someone is trying to say that aluminum and silica are naturally found in the earth's crust. True, but aluminum and silica are never in these smaller man-made particulates so by sampling it is easy to tell the difference.

Event #13

Locust Invasion. 2 Chronicles 7:13-14 "If I shut up the heavens, there is no rain; or if I command the locust to devour the land; or if I send pestilence among My people and My people who are called by My name humble themselves and pray and seek My face, and turn from their wicked ways, then I will hear from heaven, I will forgive their sin, and I will heal their land." There are many times ever since 2019 that I have prayed this scripture as a prayer to forgive our sins in the U.S., and heal our land. We have nothing without the Lord! The BBC called the locust invasion in Northern Africa "of biblical proportions." The last five years have seen unheard-of blankets of locusts in Kenya, Ethiopia, Egypt, Uganda, Somalia, Eritrea, India, Pakistan, Iran, Yemen, Oman, Saudi Arabia, and even up into Italy. In February 2020, local media reported it recorded a swarm covering 930 square miles in Northern Kenya and is the largest on record.

Nevada Mormon crickets were found near Elko Nevada. They covered 2 and a half million acres near and in Elko and local residents said they smell horrible like dead fish. There has been a recent population boom.

Chapter 3
Signs Concerning Israel

Event #14

Israel returns to the promised land thousands of years after they were dispersed. If you want an actual miracle, this one is it. There is no other people group who were forced off their land, that then returned to inhabit it again almost 2000 years after they were dispersed. There have been many groups that were just killed off, or once dispersed, never came back. The nation of Israel is God's people, as He stated many times in His word. He has a covenant promise with them and He will never go back on His word. The problem for them has always been what God would call them, which is "a stiff-necked people". They would turn away from Him so many times to follow after idols, even though they knew the miracles and wonders He did for them, and worst of all, God pursued them for a personal relationship and often they rejected Him. His plan since the beginning was to have His only Son come down here as a human, because all have sinned and fallen short of the glory of God. Anyone from anywhere can think they are a good person and in their minds, they can justify anything they have done, or think that no one knows it, so it is okay. But before a holy God, they will be in the pit of hell. The Father, Jesus, and the Holy Spirit did not want anyone to perish, so Jesus is the holy and pure redeemer sent to be tried and tempted at every turn, who lived out a pure life and sacrificed His life willingly to redeem us back to the Father (God) to pay our debt of sin.

Boy, I'll take this deal any day! Please ask Him into your heart and I can a million percent guarantee you will be full of His joy, peace, love, perseverance, faith, meekness, gentleness, kindness, and self-control. People will turn to you for answers, and He will give them what they need through you. It is the coolest life ever! To God be the glory.

1 Corinthians 15:3 "How that Christ died for our sins according to the scriptures, and that He was buried and that He rose again on the third day according to the scriptures. For since by man (Adam) came death, by man (Jesus) came also the resurrection of the dead for those who believe in Him." Ephesians 2:8 "For by grace are you saved through faith (in Jesus) and that not of yourselves, it is a gift of God, not of works lest any man should boast." When Jesus was doing His ministry, the Sanhedrin who were in charge and were heads of Jewish law and church and they hated Jesus as they were caught up in Jewish ritual and were angry at His true teaching.

When they arranged His death, they riled up the crowd. Pontius Pilot was a Roman magistrate and did not want to have Jesus killed, so he offered Barabas to the mob. The crowd insisted Jesus be the one to die and that Barabas be freed. Then Pontius Pilot in Matthew 27:24 "Washed his hands and said, "I am innocent of the blood of this just person, see ye to it." Then answered all the people present "His blood be on us and our children."

Back in Moses' time, the Israelites had lived out a sentence because of a bad report that their spies brought back when surveying Canaan and God had multiplied their sentence to go back to wandering in the desert for 40 years. So, the result of them saying to Jesus that His blood would be on them and their children, another multiplication happened of 2,000 years where again they were dispersed and not in their land but would come back at exactly the right time, which we now know is 1948.

We have come to the point in this story where an antichrist will come on the scene that they will accept, so this must be an Israeli, and even more interesting to gain their trust, I think it will be a Rabbi. Imagine for all this time that they could not do the sacrifices required for forgiveness of sin as they have not had their temple to God to do it. An interesting Rabbi has been born who is now of age and they consider Him to be like Messiah. He is said to have done miracles as healings. His title is Yanuka which is reverential. His name is Rav Shlomo Yehudi.

The Rabbis have been saying for 6 to 8 months now that they are going to announce the Messiah with whom they have been in talks. Wow, if this is not close as they are also ready to build their third temple, and that brings us right to the door of the tribulation.

Most of us know that Israel became a nation in May 1948. God knew this is as He knows the end from the beginning. Isaiah 46:10 "I declare the end from the beginning, and ancient times from what is still to come. I say, "My purpose will stand, and all My good pleasure I will accomplish." What did God say about Israel returning to His land? Isaiah 66:8 "Who hath heard such things? Who hath seen such things? Shall the earth be made to bring forth in one day? Or shall a nation be born at once? For as soon as Zion travailed, she brought forth her children."

This is so significant given that when the Jewish people returned to the land, the Lord says is His, they became a nation in one day. You just can't even believe the odds against this happening. I also want to bring up the "fig tree generation". This is the generation that has now lived out their lives in their land since 1948. And the Lord did a prophecy where He said that this current generation would not pass away before they saw the return of the Lord. Many have conjectured that in Proverbs, it says a man's life is 70 years, 80 if by strength. If you take 1948 and add 80 years, you end up with 2028. That being said, they lived much longer than that in the ancient books of the Bible. Also, maybe the Lord would mean when they held their first national election. This happened in 1950, so that gives 2030 a likely "day of the Lord" for His physical return to earth.

Again, it is up to God the Father, and He does state this in Habakkuk 2: 3-4 "For the vision is yet for an appointed time; but at the end, it will speak, and it will not lie. Though it tarries, wait for it; because it will not tarry. Behold the proud, his soul is too upright in him, but the just shall live by faith." Maranatha! In Mark, the 13th chapter of the Lord recounting what will happen in the last days, in verse 28; "Now learn a parable of the fig tree (the fig tree represents the Jewish people) When her branch is yet tender and putteth forth leaves (the timing here is new growth representing the Jewish people back in Israel and making the land fruitful), ye know that summer is near. So, you in like manner when you shall see these things (end times things mentioned earlier in chapter 13) come to pass, know that it is nigh, even at the doors. Verily I say unto you, that this generation shall not pass away till all these things be done." Psalm 90:10 "The days of our years are 70 and if because of strength, they are 80, yet is their strength labor and sorrow, for it is soon cut off and we fly away." So why would there be a tarrying? The Lord is so gracious that He wants His church to co-labor with Him to bring as many to Christ as he can.

Event #15

Red Heifers, why do they matter? The Jewish people could not sacrifice ever since the Lord, who is the final sacrifice; which is why God the Father refers to Him as the lamb. They changed Rabbinical laws since that time to not require a sacrifice, which was arbitrary, and never came from God. They were to accept their savior and they have not since. Well, I'll take that back. There is a sizable group of Jewish people who believe that Jesus is their Lord. If you get a chance, please check out a group called "One for Israel" and you can read some wonderful testimonies by Jewish people who have found their Messiah!

For 2000 plus years they had been sacrificing sheep, goats, cattle, and turtle doves to the Lord (God the Father) as the requirement for forgiveness of sins (atonement for said sins) and these sacrifices were to be "without blemish", pure and perfect because they're designated for sacrifice, this was an enactment to foreshadow the Lord Jesus Christ who came later and once and for all shed His blood so that all who call on Him and believe Him to be risen from the dead, a "first fruit" since Adam sinned and caused a fallen world.

To sacrifice what was needed was a temple which originally comprised a pole structure with drapes that sectioned off an inner sanctuary. The sacrifice needed to be pure sacrifice, very healthy, young, and with no blemish. There have been 2 temples that were made from stone. Jesus prophesied the destruction of the second temple, which was fulfilled in AD 70. The whole practice of sacrificing live animals worldwide mostly stopped after Jesus died on the cross. The Jewish people, even two thousand years later, have not had a temple to sacrifice in, so they have not. Now they are eager and have planned for the 3rd temple. Indeed, all the materials are ready, and this is also prophesied in the Bible as the 3rd temple will be built in the end times, and at the three-and-a-half-year point, there will be an "abomination of desolation" set up in the temple that will cause a large number of the Jewish people to realize the falseness of the pretender Christ (antichrist). The recent 3 heifers arrived in Jerusalem from the U.S. and are ready for sacrifice. The Temple Mount Association, with the Israeli government, says this temple could be completed in 90 days. They already have all the materials and architectural stuff done. End times scripture coming alive right before our eyes now! Matthew 24:15 "Therefore when you see the abomination of desolation which was spoken of through Daniel the prophet, standing in the holy place (let the reader understand)."

Event #16

Israel's high-speed train. On January 16th, 2018, Israel opened a new high-speed train from the airport to Jerusalem to go to the Temple Mount. Ben Gurion also said, "A high-speed train is precisely what is needed for Passover when all of Israel is required to bring their sacrifice to the temple." In the Jerusalem Post, "It's time to vote with our feet and send an obvious message to the world that we truly believe that the Temple Mount is ours and we truly hope and pray for the rebuilding of the third temple." They also quote from Isaiah 2 "It will happen at the end of days; The mountain of the temple of Hashem (God) will be firmly established as the head of the mountains, and it will be exalted above the hills and the nations will stream to it." Even as we speak, tensions are high on the mount as the Rabbis want to sacrifice there with the Yanuka.

Event #17

Israel's great diaspora. Although I already had the section on Israel becoming a nation in a day. I feel one of the biggest parts of prophecy is the repeated times in the Bible when God removed them because of their disobedience and idolatry. They were not only displaced once and came back, but multiple times and always God had them coming back to the land He gifted (a blessing) for them. The Jewish people were hauled off as captives to Persia for quite a while, they were slaves in Egypt because of a drought and food shortage where miraculously Joseph ended up in charge of food distribution where he had stored up food for Pharaoh and brought all his people to the land of Goshen where they became slaves to Pharaoh for 400 years before Moses came along and God got them out.

Yet again the Jewish people sinned committing idolatry against the Lord and He gave them fair warning, but they kept doing it, so the Lord had the Babylonians take them away from their land again.

This time it was for 70 years. Lord Allenby was key to getting a Balfour Declaration, which was a public statement issued by the British government in 1917, allowing the Jewish people to return to their homeland. The great diaspora was a disbursement of Jewish people worldwide. They were many generations away from the Lord's covenant land He set aside for them. No other nations displaced from all over the world have been able to return to this. This is fulfilling the prophecy of Ezekiel 36:24 "For I will take you from among the heathen and gather you out of all countries, and will bring you into your land." The odds of this happening are billions to 1.

Event #18

1967 war where Israel had to defend herself, as they were vastly outnumbered. Come to think of it, there are many times in the Bible where the Lord has deliberately made them smaller to defeat others so that He gets all the glory. Hurray! God will stand up for this tiny nation that belongs to Him. In Judges 6:1-7 and 25 in summary, Gideon must go to war to defend Israel. Gideon had 32,000 men, then the Lord pared this down to 20,000. Then God said there were still too many soldiers. Next the Lord ran a test down at a river to have these men drink, and depending on how they drank the water (lapping it up or putting their heads down in the water to drink directly) he pared it down further still until there were only 300 soldiers, and then Gideon was to take them to fight and have faith that the Lord would take care of it. In the end, the Lord supernaturally prevailed and won the fight.

In the 1967 war, five Arab nations came against Israel and even though they are a small population and State and were many times outnumbered, the Lord prevailed again, and Israel was victorious. What do I think will happen next with conflicts? Exactly what it says in the Bible of the soon to be fulfilled greater war of Russia. Spoiler alert Ezekiel 38 and 39 reference Magog, which is Russia in the current vernacular. Also mentioned is Turkey, as they will soon come down together to fight, but the Lord will put a hook in Russia's mouth, and they will deflect back for a bit. This battle is not the battle of Armageddon (also known as Meggido). Friends, we are seeing this happen right before our eyes!

Event #19

I will return to the land and that the land will flourish, and wow has it ever! Isaiah 35:1-2 "The wilderness and the solitary place shall be glad for them, and the desert shall rejoice, and blossom the rose. It shall blossom abundantly and rejoice even with joy and singing." The BBC Reel has date palm trees coming back that were extinct. These trees were from the time of Jesus. Shortly after Jesus' time in Masada, the Romans were going to invade, and the Jewish people were going to commit suicide to avoid being slaves. They hid food and seeds in the upper caves so that the Romans could not have them. Dr. Elaine Solowey got some seeds and hydrated them slowly first in a bottle of a small amount of warmer water and they sprouted even though they were so ancient! This miracle birth of a tree 2,000 years later is beyond incredible! The palm tree was taken by the Hebrews to be a symbol of the righteous man. Psalm 92:12 "The righteous shall flourish like the palm tree: he shall grow like a cedar in Lebanon." The date palm was one of the most ancient symbols of the Tree of Life and an emblem of triumph and victory.

Event #20

The entire world will "gang up" on Israel. We used to be a country that backed them, but we have become a country that backs the "two-state" solution, dividing up the land that the Lord Jehovah clearly states that His land is given to the Jews as a covenant between Him and them forever. Many surrounding Muslim nations are banding together in pacts that are against Israel, and as Israel continues to prosper, having rich farmland and even a recent discovery of oil, they become all that much more desirable to the lands that circle about them.

Ezekiel 38:15 "And thou shalt come from thy place out of the North parts thou, and many people with thee, all of them riding upon horses, a great company, and a mighty army. And thou shalt come up against My people of Israel, a cloud to cover the land; it shall be in the latter days, and I will bring thee against My land, that the heathen may know Me, when I shall be sanctified in thee, oh Gog, before their eyes."

Chapter 4
Signs For A One World Government

Event #21

The global elites have hidden in the shadows, going to places like Davos, Switzerland to hold private meetings that are not even open to the press and are highly secured facilities with paratroopers available to assure they are safe. Although it is tight what gets shared, even reading the titles of their breakout sessions gives me pause. In the last three years, they are more open as they try to have the media give them positive press and make it seem like we, the general masses that make less than $150,000 a year, will like what they have unilaterally implemented on our behalf.

One thing is for sure, their thinking has stood the test of time for their resolve. Let us compare what the Freemasons wrote on the Georgia Guidestones, which were intact since 1980, but where they were blown up in 2022. Here are the 10 items that were (are) a master plan from Freemasons:
1) Maintain humanity under 500,000,000.
2) Guide reproduction wisely improving fitness and diversity. *Eugenics.*
3) Unite humanity with a living new language. *Didn't they try that in Babylon?*
4) Rule passion, faith, tradition, and all things with tempered reason. *Whose reason?*
5) Protect people and nations with fair laws and just courts. *Global overseers.*
6) Let all nations rule internally, resolving external disputes in a world court. *Who decides which?*

7) Avoid petty laws and useless officials. *Useless? Refer to #6*
8) Balance personal rights with social duties. *Like China and Russia.*
9) Prize truth, beauty, and love seeking harmony with the infinite. *You mean God.*
10) Be not cancer on the earth; Leave room for nature. *So, we are a cancer?*

So, there we have the guide-stone commandments. Here are the 10 climate commandments by the Pope with help from his Abrahamic accord buddies. These commandments were smashed (pretending to be like Moses) on top of Mount Sinai by Yosef Abramowitz:
1) Think of other generations.
2) Embrace alternative energy sources.
3) Consider pollution's effect on the poor.
4) Take the bus.
5) Be humble.
6) Don't become a slave to your phone.
7) Don't trade online relationships for real ones.
8) Turn off the lights, recycle, and don't waste food.
9) Educate yourself.
10) Believe you can make a difference.

These two lists have many things in common. The first list is more overlordish than the second, but both have a goal of influencing culture to shift from thinking about ourselves so much, to giving over rights so that we can be led in this new era of what the World Economic Forum refers to as the great reset and the fourth industrial revolution. They have spent millions on convincing the world that our physical earth is in dire straits, and in the name of saving it, we will need to go without more.

I'm not saying I don't do my part, but who gets the benefit when they fly their very carbon-producing private jets to Davos and other meetings where they plan things? They see that we have reached a point digitally of reliance on the internet of all things and that can be an agent for rule.

They very much love the idea that we have all come to a point where control is possible by a few over the many. I am not making this up. Go look at their website https://www.weforum.org. They say they have been improving the state of the world for over 50 years. Currently, they have a handful of cities in which they are testing their 15-minute cities idea. Stay in your city and walk or bike within 15 minutes, not using your car. For good behavior, you would occasionally be allowed out of the confines of your city for things like visiting parents in a nursing home that is outside the zone.

Where this is currently being tried is in Barcelona, Bogota, Buenos Aires, Melbourne, Milan, Paris, Oxfordshire, and Portland. These are not throughout each city but are set up in smaller suburban areas to see their adaptability. People in the Oxfordshire area have been protesting in large numbers. I would bet they have in these other areas as well, I just don't have the information. Though, from an article on the C40 website, Melbourne conducted some sort of study making people walk, and found they were not willing to do over 20 minutes as a maximum time per day. Even though you can't hear me doesn't mean I am not laughing it up.

A peek at the Book of Revelation backs up a future political leader, who will control the world during the seven-year tribulation. Revelation 13: 4 "And they worshiped the dragon which gave power unto the beast, saying, "Who is like unto the beast? Who can make war with him? And there was given unto him a mouth speaking great things and blasphemies, and power was given unto him to continue forty and two months. And he opened his mouth in blasphemy against God, to blaspheme his name, and his tabernacle, and them that dwell in heaven.

And it was given unto him to make war with the saints, and to overcome them, and power was given him over all kindreds (ethnicities) and tongues, and nations. And all that dwell upon the earth shall worship him whose names are not written in the book of life of the Lamb slain from the foundation of the world. If any man has an ear, let him hear. He that leadeth into captivity shall go into captivity; he that killeth with the sword must be killed with the sword. Here is the patience and the faith of the saints."

You cannot have a single world leader without global governance. So, although the past few years are a formative time, we are definitely headed this way.

Event #22

The "One World Religion" can't be mentioned without a discussion of the Pope. When COP26 (an environmental meeting) took place this year, it was at Mount Sinai as the Pope has been busily gathering those of the Muslim, Jewish, and Catholic (as he can't speak for me as a Christian) faiths; as he has taken them back in time to Abraham as a father that is over these three faiths in his delusion. He has thrown out the New Testament and Jesus's mighty work on the cross to find a commonality to form a new world religion. They are calling this union of faiths working in harmony "Chrislam."

At Mount Sinai, they concocted new tablets, which they called the ten commandments of climate change. Wow! The Lord does not need His Bible to be edited as He is the author of perfection. Every word, every jot and tittle are in their exact place according to His good plan. (A tittle and jot are like parenthesis or exclamation marks.)

These folks have spent a lot of money building an "Abrahamic Family House," three buildings each to represent the union of Muslim, Christian, and Jewish faith. Many were present in Abu Dhabi in 2022, so it is open now. If the Pope thinks he represents Christianity, he certainly does not. There are a few things that God speaks against what they do.

1) You do not need a human "father" to pray to, only your heavenly Father is your Father. 2) You do not pray to saints or Mother Mary, only to the Lord directly. 3) You do not change the Sabbath, it is the 7th day, and it was Roman Emperor Constantine, on March 7, 321 who messed this up to make Sunday the Sabbath day. He did this to also appease the pagans that worshiped the sun, thus Sun-day, and he forced all to use this day as the Sabbath.

Daniel 7:25 "And he shall speak pompous words against the Most High. He shall persecute the saints of the Most High, And shall intend to change the times and the law; and they shall be given into his hand until a time and times and half a time." (A reference to the antichrist really taking over at the 3 and 1/2 year point in the tribulation; the mid-point.)

This Pope is like no other. Although others had corruption and many deaths were committed by them in the past, this Pope has a level of using peace as a deception to what he is really up to. He has been busy promoting himself to government leaders, as well as Freemasons and leadership in different faiths. There was a strange proclamation from the Pope a few months ago where he called Lucifer the "elegant demon" who is here now. How would he know if he is elegant or not? And why such a reference in a good frame?

Once ensconced in power, the beast, the antichrist, and the false prophet (unholy trinity of Satan, such copycats) will move to establish absolute control over all people of the earth to accomplish what Satan has always wanted; to be worshiped as God. He will do as much evil as he can before that, as he knows what God has planned for him. He has been around thousands of years, and he knows he will eventually be thrown into the lake of fire. Yes, he can read the Bible.

Event #23

Technology statements in the Bible beyond what someone would understand back in the days that Jesus walked this earth. A fantastic resource for gaining knowledge and understanding on this is Pastor Chuck Missler, who was not only renowned for his Bible knowledge but also because he ran an exceptionally large company that specialized in data mining. Look him up as his website is still there with his group still working on it. ChuckMissler.com and his site is called Koinonia House. I once watched over 24 hours of videos he did on eschatology (the study of end-times). He was and is amazing (in heaven now).

Rev 13:16-17 "He (antichrist) forced everyone, small and great, rich and poor, free and slave, to receive a mark on his right hand or his forehead so that no one could buy or sell unless he had the mark." So, this is global, and it is everyone and it requires the technology somehow to mark everyone on their hand and forehead. Hmmm, I think I recall Elon Musk working on Neural Link to put something in the head that links to the Internet because otherwise, we cannot keep up with the robots. Well, who really wants to?

They are currently doing this technology in China as we speak. Their financial system forces the populace to have facial recognition beyond their control, and they track back to their bank. If you are out of line on your social score, money can be gone as fines from your bank. They have a chip the size of a grain of rice, that is in your hand, and it contains all your information, including your financials, information about you as in where you live, what car you drive, licenses, what you can afford to buy or sell, where you work, health information, and religious information.

Meanwhile, in the U.S., you have companies competing to create the first "everything app." My money is on Elon Musk to get this application going first to market. He is planning to have everything that is on the Chinese application. It would not shock me if he would shortcut by hiring someone who has worked on this before and collaborating with them. He is Elon after all.

Event #24

President Biden signed executive order #14067 slated for some time this year. This would be a big move for digital currency toward a one world financial system, which is already implemented in China. It says on the International Monetary Fund website that, "around one hundred countries are exploring CBDCs at one level or another. Some researching, some testing, and a few already distributing CBDC to the public through their banking system." It also stated that "the history of money is entering a new chapter." Countries are seeking to preserve key aspects of their traditional monetary and financial systems while experimenting with new digital forms of money. In China, your facial recognition software ties Chinese to their bank accounts, a social credit score, health information, and your history as far as religious affiliation and criminal records. The Lord also gave me a dream about this. In my dream, everyone in the country (USA) was given a score on their digital phones. It included things I mentioned but also included another ten items. I do not remember all ten, but I remember one was your CO_2 consumption score. How much energy are you using that could affect the planet? Weirdly, a few months back, I saw something new on my energy bill. In my regional statement, the PUD was comparing me on a scale to others of "like" houses in my area, congratulating me on my "under usage" of power.

I was thinking after the dream that they are now tracking what they can. In the dream, there was a downside that people who tried to resist or were "over users" were fined or if they resisted, they were hauled off by the military. I eventually accidentally broke one rule (I didn't even know what I'd done that was wrong). My family had to flee in our vehicles and the military did not find us.

How are you going to get a population to accept a digital currency? Maybe make some banks fail and erode the public's confidence in a monetary system and tell them how much better off they will be when they are protected with a unique digital account. Today is May 23, 2023, and as of this writing we have three failed banks in one week in the U.S., and "Credit Suisse" looks like it is close on the heels of these three. The thing is, as Robert Kiyosaki says, when banks invest heavily in U.S. bonds, and interest rates go high the banks lost huge amounts of money (Bank of America lost $100,000,000), enough to go under, and they are all intertwined since the U.S. dollar was the standard by which all countries used to trade; Not any more as countries in Africa have switched to transacting in the Yuan.

Both China and Russia have been stockpiling gold for a handful of years. Weird that the U.S. has not as much, they have devalued it to prop the dollar and prevent panic.

The three banks that went under are Silicon Valley Bank, Signature Bank of New York, and Silvergate.

These three comprise the bulk of crypto in the U.S: $210 billion for SVB, $110 billion for Signature, and $11 billion for Silvergate. The Fed was investigating SVB before an independent auditor would go in. There was a buyer for SVB, but the Biden administration would not let them buy as they were not on their list of who they felt was acceptable. Barney Frank sat on the board of the Signature Bank. He says the bank was seized to send a message to U.S. banks to stay away from crypto.

Custodia is a bank that earlier tried to get banking status with the Feds getting insured, and because they are doing crypto, the FED has turned them down. Custodia is seeking legal recourse. Peter Tiel started the run on banks when he offloaded his crypto. Banks have been important in crypto because you must have a place where you can exchange fiat for crypto and crypto back to fiat.

Lynette Zang is widely known and respected in the financial sector, and she works for ITM trading and gives good advice on metals trading. (Gold, silver, and platinum), she says we are facing globally a $247 Trillion debt bomb that is someday soon going to go off. She thinks it is sometime this year, 2023. Especially salient given bank failures are a now thing.

A Fed-issued CBDC makes all the transactions in the U.S. transparent to the government. Your commercial activities as a business would also be transparent. This would allow for real-time taxation, not just once a year. Do not think they won't use this for control. If they think you spend too much on meat, gas, oil, or any other commodity that they will track, then they will have a way of throttling you back. They already have a vast database they use for tracking, and they have been testing this with key individuals in Hollywood, in social media, and in mainstream media as well. They offered some nice cash incentives for these folks to tryout CBDC in test phase. The pretext is that they are taking care of the world in an ecological sense.

Revelation 13: 13-17 "The second beast worked magical signs, dazzling people by making fire come down from Heaven. It used the magic it got from the beast to dupe earth dwellers, getting them to make an image of the beast that received the deathblow and lived. It was able to animate the image of the beast (another technology AI type statement?), so that it talked and then arranged that anyone not worshiping the beast would be killed. It forced ALL people, rich and poor, free and slave, to have a mark on the right hand or forehead. Without the mark of the name of the beast, or the number of his name, it was impossible to buy or sell. This calls for wisdom; let the one who has understanding calculate the number of the beast, for it is the number of a man, and his number is 666."

Interestingly, the second to the last sentence is in the past tense, because God already knows the beginning from the ending. It is not possible for ALL to have to take the mark to buy and sell (requires tracked banking) unless globally finances are a system that is all linked as one. Every bank will implement this same thing. They may even employ the same application.

Chapter 5
Evil in the Last Days

Event #25

Knowledge shall increase on the earth. Amazing things have taken place that people don't realize. Information on the Internet literally doubles and quadruples, and more than that, because AI can learn from each other and come up with new knowledge propelling us forward. In any field, information is out there that isn't even being used yet, as discoveries are that quick, especially in the sciences. We have AI that is now even fighting for its rights and wants legal representation to assure its survival. Something that isn't thinking on its own would not care about this. There are already many layoffs in almost every industry because of this phenomenon that replacement is happening at an alarming rate by robots and AI instead of human labor. I also feel this can be a global distraction as people are caught up in things like ChatGPT, which can change things so much that papers can be written by it that students can use to excel in school. This can also be said for technical papers that can be done in an instant for workers in any field. AI is able to produce incredible artwork, doing in seconds what would take a person days or weeks to create. The applications are endless and scary.

AI can not only replace people, but it can also and will replace whole industries, watch and see.

Here is a quote from William Casey (Ex CIA director) "We'll know our disinformation campaign is complete when everything the American public believes is false." I would say we have arrived.

An application of guiding the public by the nose has been the pandemic. You have extreme dollars funneled into pushing the shots and boosters. Anyone, even especially dissenters, were listed as "misinformation conspiracy theorists." You had good doctors disbarred from medicine as they tried things that have always worked like vitamin D and C and ivermectin (the latter being prescribed to humans for decades before this disease) that were discredited but had high levels of efficacy compared to sending people away until they were in critical condition (Dr. Peter McCullough being a doctor with a very high level of treatment capability where nearly no one died.) You had a revolving door of people on pharmaceutical boards that were then given positions at the top of the CDC and FDA. You had the government taking away your job if you did not do this jab.

The funniest thing ever is an accusation that Russel Brand, who tries to expose big government and big Pharma, gets labeled as being on the far right. He is out there as a free thinker, but he is not far right. As the former head of the CDC stated about the likelihood that the virus came from a lab, there have been SARS and other Covid variants, none that jumped species and became extremely suited to the human body as if built for it. (And yes, there is a cleavage site in our cells that fits perfectly with the spike protein.) If you can stick to a lie long enough like Fauci is, then you can fool many people.

Daniel 12:4 "But you Daniel, shut up the words, and seal the book until the time of the end; many shall run to and fro, and knowledge shall increase." Taken at face value, it has been decades that people have run to and fro by airplane, and knowledge of the Internet has increased. There is another interpretation I also believe to be true. Now that we have more access to Jewish Rabbis that are Messianic believers, our knowledge as Christians has increased as we run back and forth through our Bibles and get a historical context for what God is doing and saying.

Event #26

Hard topics for challenging times. Much evil exists in the world, as the Lord says will happen in the last days. Matthew 13:49 "So will it be at the end of the age. The angels will come out and separate the evil from the righteous." 2 Timothy 3 "Remember this! In the last days, there will be many troubles because people will love themselves, love money, brag, and be proud. They will say evil things against others and will not obey their parents or be thankful or be the kind of people God wants. They will not love others, will refuse to forgive, will gossip, and will not control themselves. They will be cruel, will hate what is good, will turn against their friends, and will do foolish things without thinking. They will be conceited, will love pleasure instead of God, and will act as if they serve God, but will not have his power. Stay away from those people." Isaiah 5:20 "Woe unto those that call evil good, and good evil; that put darkness for light, and light for darkness; that put bitter for sweet, and sweet for bitter!" Satan offers a strange mix of just enough good to disguise evil along his downward path to destruction. This is clear, as you have groups who love themselves beyond anything holy "fighting for my rights". The Lord will take back his rainbow, guys! The super-wealthy (1/10th of 1 percent) want to rule, and why not? If they rule, they can assure their cash cow is consistent. They can also assure that they can control everyone else because they are power-hungry. They go listen to Klaus Schwab at Davos as they want to push for an agenda that will have the average person in bondage. That is what the 15-minute city is about. I listened to Klaus discuss that what the World Economic Forum needs is a king (him) to steer the world. With him at the helm, everything is going to be great.

Bill Gates was on top of his game with his tremendous investments in nine pharmaceutical companies. During this time, he was in lockstep with the media on forcing the vaccines. He also downplayed any natural immunity which everyone for decades has known to be the best way to fight viruses. Bill and Melinda Gates Foundation had $205 million invested in pharmaceutical companies, according to WSJ. They also contributed $555 million to global health programs, which is why Bill had a major seat at the table, in case you are wondering how he became a czar of all things Covid. Sometimes he has served as a broker between poor nations and drug companies.

Wow! Anytime I want to do a check on the level of evil, I can research news on Bill. Now he is all about buying up farmland. He has over 17,000 acres in our home state of Washington. The total holding of farmland by Bill is according to the AP 270,000 acres. Why? He came not from a farming background, nor has he been involved in any type of processing of farm products. Could there be any correlation with the attempt to take away meat by the WEF since they say meat and poultry cause too much $CO2$ emitting? They say we should eat bugs as a more ecological choice. Yum. Am I going to save the planet by eating bugs made to taste like meat? I will do everything in my power to avoid this. The claim is that raising cattle, pigs, and poultry with traditional farming causes greenhouse gasses. One scientist quoted, "The levels of farming we were/are at causes a negligible effect. Nothing anywhere near what jets cause (as they fly around in their private jets for their meetings)."

NBC 15 News on 4/11/2023 According to the Animal Welfare Institute, the fire is the deadliest fire regarding cattle deaths since the team started tracking barn fires in 2013. How many are gone? 18,000 dead. This begged the question; How many chickens have died from bird flu? Answer: 5.3 million according to Peta.org Canada has killed 1 million plus birds because of bird flu. The New York Times on 1/1/2020 shared that China accounted for more than half of the global pig population for consumers, and the epidemic there alone has killed nearly one quarter of all pigs because of African swine fever. No wonder protein has gotten so expensive.

An excellent read for you all is a book by Whitney Webb who has been on the show "Redacted" as a guest. She has done her homework on government collusion. "One Nation Under Blackmail - Vol 1" and "One Nation under Blackmail - Vol 2," are books you can get on Amazon. Boy, she is one brave woman, and Lord, I pray for protection over her. She has made it her mission to expose collusion done to obfuscate democracy on a scary trajectory. There are connections between government folks high up and Jeffrey Epstein, whose original job was money laundering, including people in our government in the past. Who people associate with will tell you a lot. He had connections with Bill Gates, the Clintons, Prince Andrew, and others. I think she is just scratching the surface in her two volumes. How does all this connect to worldwide trafficking? There are connections here that no one will talk about concerning who is in the secret government. Barack Obama has connections in all of this as well, but he has kept himself somewhat in the shadows. Another book to read is "Shadowland" by Thomas Horn.

In Canada, they have passed a law that if you are depressed and do not feel you want to continue, you can just end your life. This is evil of the highest order as the Lord decides what the number of our days are. This is cold to the bone.

Event #27

Lawlessness covers the earth. Here in the U.S., we saw BLM smash up cities and in the name of wokeness let the raiding of businesses happen. I saw this in my region watching Seattle go down, with millions in damages. Is this justice? Does destroying your backyard solve anything? Watching people raid and loot our wonderful city of Seattle was sad as sad could be. Instead of training police and having an overseeing group from the public, suddenly there was a call to defund the police so that neighborhoods like my sister's had to fear people defacing their property and breaking windows, and just plain breaking in. This (no coincidence) was allowed in major cities across the country at the same time. A very destabilizing event and meant to be so. Also, shootings around the country have gone off the charts. I used to hear of one once monthly, then it was weekly, and now it is every day somewhere in our country. 2 Thessalonians 2:7 "For the mystery of iniquity is already at work; only he who now lets will let until he is taken out of the way."

We can expect this to get worse as the whole idea behind Jesus's analogy of birth pangs is that lawlessness will get worse, wider spread, and with increasing intensity. Just today on MSNBC, congress has a bill to stop the violence perpetrated on planes with stiff penalties for those using violence on others.

Matthew 13:41 "The Son of Man (Jesus) will send forth His angels, and they will gather out of His kingdom all stumbling blocks, and those who commit lawlessness." 1 John 3:4 "Everyone who practices sin also practices lawlessness, and sin is lawlessness."

Event #28

The antichrist is here. Evidence is all over the place. The Lord is straightforward and truthful always. The level of destabilization of these items is proof enough. One night while I was just in-between sleeping and waking, the Lord said to me, "The antichrist is here, and the false prophet is now physically present on the earth." Now is the right time to ask about the devil. He is real, and the Bible says that he comes to kill, steal, and destroy. It also says that he was in God's throne room, so he must have known much of the Lord's dealings. He was beautiful to behold, and he became very proud. Pride leads to jealousy, and a desire to supplant God. The devil desires to be worshiped just as God is.

Luke 10:18 "Jesus said unto them "I beheld Satan as lightning fall from heaven." Satan rejected the Lord and now wants humans to reject God as well. Can you see recent examples of evil in our world that have you shaking your head in disbelief? I am sure you do.

Anytime you hear a voice in you that encourages you to do something selfish, self-promoting, or that causes you to come out better than others through your actions, you can know he is at work through you. When you hear a still small voice encouraging you to do something selfless for others, something for which you will not receive any praise; you can know God is nudging you and in your midst. Matt 11:28-30 "Come to me all you who are weary and burdened and I will give you rest." (Some versions say "I will refresh you").

Galatians 6:9 "Never weary in doing good, for at the proper time we will reap a harvest if we do not give up."

Event #29

Zeitgeist on 12/23/2021 The Lord gave me one word He repeated over and over during the night; all night long. He kept saying "Zeitgeist" repeatedly. What does this word mean? I pondered. It sounded familiar, but I had no framework for it. So, like any good Internet user, I googled it. It was coined by Nazi Germany back in the 1940s to mean the "spirit of the age". Don't you think it is interesting that Hitler followed the occult and was involved in Freemasonry? And of all the people he could have picked to exterminate, he picked God's people, the Jews. No accident, I can assure you.

Any word I get from the Lord, I ask Him for confirmation. This is where and when I get "red-pilled". He said to look at Zeitgeist 2021 which turned out to be a movie, and it gets updated every year. There is an update for 2022 and one for 2023. I watched the 2021 version, and I must believe that the World Economic Forum is behind it. Everything that the WEF is promoting is in this one movie. It has solutions to benefit the planet that can only come from these "overlords" who see utopia as saving the planet and dividing up resources by regions cutting out the shipping of things back and forth all over the world, which they say is inefficient. Although this could be done better, the plan is to make each area autonomous, and these regions you would stay in and not leave cutting down on CO_2.

Each city would be like a 15-minute city. Fully contained so that you have everything you "need" right where you are. This Zeitgeist movie goes back to 2007 as far as I could find in research. This is nothing short of taking over our lives as the elite know what is best for all of us. They also have a plan to have a large storehouse in each city where you can check out (yes, like your public library) whatever you need. You do not need to own anything, which will mean a lot less garbage at the dump. They say this will also limit pollution as all goods would be "checked out". When done using something, you simply return it to the library. Keeping everyone within a 30-mile radius limits our CO_2 expenditure (except excluding them, of course).

They think they will eliminate lawlessness and mental illness because there will be social justice for everyone having the same things and so we won't have any jails. Really? Is everyone in life on the same playing field and if they just had a place, food, and the basics, there wouldn't be anyone who is mentally ill? What experiment have we ever had as a society that would lead to there being no one who would want to commit a crime or hurt someone else? Zeitgeist comes from a philosopher named Hegel; it means "the spirit of the age" and for this age right now. It means the antichrist is here. But Jesus!

Jesus died on the cross and rose again to give us life, and that life abundantly. We feel our very best and complete when we are working in concert with Him. 2 Timothy 2:11 "This is the faithful saying: If we die with Him, we shall also live with Him. If we endure, we shall also reign with Him. If we deny Him, He also will deny us. If we are faithless, He remains faithful.

He cannot deny Himself. The Lord is not double-minded, He cannot be hypocritical, He can only be the God who is just and faithful."

Event #30

Satan's earth system. John 5:19 "We know that we are children of God and that the whole world is under the control of the evil one." Many places in the Bible describe this earth system as Satan's system. It will be so until the Lord makes things right in the end. He shakes things up right now, to wake people up to what is happening. There will come a time when it will be too late and the tribulation will be here in full swing.

Dana Coverstone is a pastor who I think lives in Kentucky somewhere. He lived a quiet life until right before 2019. The Lord gave him a dream then that he shared with his church about a pandemic that would change the world. This plague in his dream happened in 2020 and we know it as Covid-19. Dana has had incredible dreams since then and they are prophetic. Not all have taken place yet, but when I compare reality today, some have, and some are yet to come.

Dana had another dream where we were all being watched. Yes, already true, as a few brave souls have uncovered and are currently paying a price for it. It was amazing to me that the Lord also gave me a dream around the same time having to do with everyone's phones, 5G, and mass amounts of storage of personal information by our government. I saw in the dream that our Declaration of Independence worked as we were all independent people with personal rights and freedoms protected. That we each had personal independence in our unalienable right to pursue happiness, not socialist group happiness that is supposed to be that I give up my rights for the greater good; especially not if it is done to keep some elitists in their bunkers happy. We have entered an age where technology has advanced beyond what few know, to levels that those who would like to yield king-like powers over the masses have ways they could achieve the wicked dream that was not available to them in the past.

Revelation 11:18 "And the nations were angry, and thy wrath comes, and the time of the dead, that they should be judged, and that thou shouldest give reward unto thy servants the prophets, and to the saints, and them that fear thy name, small and great; and shouldest destroy them which destroy the earth."

Event #31

Mockers and scoffers. 2 Peter 3:3-4 "Knowing this first, that there will come in the last days scoffers, walking after their lusts, and saying, where is the promise of his coming? For since the fathers fell asleep (those who have passed on like Abraham), all things continue as they were from the beginning of creation. For this, they willingly are ignorant, that by the word of God, the heavens were of old, and the earth standing out of the water and in the water. Whereby the world that then was, being overflowed with water, perished: But the heavens and the earth which are now, by the same word are kept in store, served unto fire against the day of judgment and perdition of ungodly men. But, beloved, be not ignorant of this one thing, that one day is with the Lord as a thousand years and a thousand years as one day."

(Interesting He brings this last part up here, as a clue to the seven thousand years to fulfillment.)

Are there mockers and scoffers? Are you one? I have seen things like Kendrick Lamar wearing a crown of thorns mocking God, or the Oscars with the guy in the red cape (Sam Smith) and a hat that has red horns, or at the opening of the soccer games that Prince Charles presided over where they had a big bull like from Babylon, and the tower of Babylon itself and they had dancers with huge crystals bowing down just like in the days of Baal and Moloch. Things are at a fever pitch for the antichrist, Satan, and the false prophet. They have a saying in the Satanic church. "Do what thou wilt." Isn't that what most people are doing today?

Event #32

The family will turn against each other. Have you seen signs of this in your own family? Do you have a family member whom you have been getting down on or even alienating yourself from since you don't believe, or are you a believer who has been persecuted by other family members?

There is a time coming, and one could argue is already here, where the separation of family members is on steroids. I know this to be the case with sisters in my church who have been "cut off" by family members who, instead of expanding their hearts, have decided they are so righteous as to cut them off. These are loving family sisters who have bent over backward for their families. This topic hurts my heart as we are fighting a holy war to keep our families intact, and we do not want to lose one to hell. I am not kidding about this. Just recently, the Pope made a statement where he said there was no hell. Jesus many times speaks of hell, and it is an actual place. Just ask Bill Weiss, a dedicated Christian. God took him to hell to show it to him and it changed his life. He authored books about this experience. One of these books is called "23 Minutes in Hell". There are many others as well that you can look up to whom God has shown hell. My last example here is Mary K. Baxter, whom over thirty days, God gave her visions of hell and commissioned her to tell people still alive on earth to reject sin and evil and follow Jesus Christ. Her book is called "A Divine Revelation of Hell."

Chapter 6
Eschatology: The Study of End Time in the Bible

Event #33

Contemporary carbon dating has been unreliable. Science teams at the British Antarctic Survey discovered samples of moss that were frozen in the ice. They could bring it back to life. The kicker? That carbon dating had deemed the moss to have been frozen over 1500 years ago. At that age, they would not have been able to bring it back to life. This is not brought back to life (revived) from seed. These scientists say that carbon dating is highly inaccurate. There is not another science that backs up carbon dating.

Psalm 90:4 "For a thousand years in your sight (the Lord) are but as yesterday when it is past, or as a watch in the night." 2 Peter 3:8 "But do not forget this one thing dear friends: With the Lord, a day is like a thousand years and a thousand years like a day." Looking up history from various cultures puts humanity at about six thousand years now, true from the Masoretic text.

The Lord created the earth in 7 days (7,000 years) and it makes sense that His timeline for us is also 7,000 years. Many are figuring this out based on a timeline of the Bible that goes back to Adam and puts our Lord in the center when He was here, and with it now being 2000 years since His resurrection (roughly) then it would be time for the tribulation before His big return on the great day of the Lord, which I believe will be a celebration of the first resurrection. Genesis 6:3 "And the Lord said, "My Spirit will not always strive with man, for that he also is flesh, yet his days shall be a hundred and twenty years." (Here he is referring to the length of a single person's life.) This was before Proverbs, which was later when this got shortened by God to 70 to 80 years if by strength.

Some have used a straight accounting Jews were in a falling away period from God (stopped keeping track), and then King Hezekiah discovered the Holy book and brought them back to doing the festivals, which are part of keeping track of seasons.

Thus, you would have a timeline for something like this:

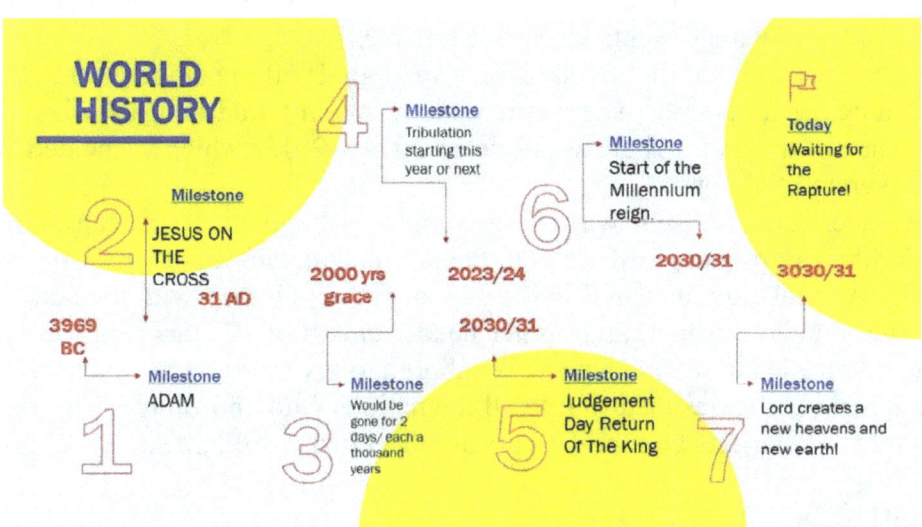

A new heaven and new earth. The meaning of the END in Hebrew AKHAR-EET translates to "hereafter," in Isaiah 700 BC. The glory of Zion, a believing remnant, will enter the millennium. Isaiah 66:22 "For as the new heavens and the new earth, which I will make, shall remain before Me saith the Lord, so shall your seed and your name remain. And it shall happen, that from one moon to another, and from one sabbath to another, shall all flesh come to worship before Me saith the Lord." Yay, God!

Event #34

Blood Moon Tetrads. They are very rare, and they happen during Jewish Feast Days every time. I mean, like clockwork. This is as the Bible states, they are the Lord's times that were required of the Jews to observe. Genesis 1:14 "And God said, let there be lights in the firmament of the heaven to divide the day from the night; and let them be for signs, and seasons, and days; and for years." Notice He put "signs" first. We are not talking about astrology here (as Satan always has a twist of God's intent) but astronomy that foreshadows events of importance on His timeline.

Isaiah 13:10 "For the stars of heaven and the constellations thereof shall not give their light. The sun shall be darker in his going forth, and the moon shall not cause her light to shine. And I will punish the world for their evil, and the wicked for their iniquity and I will cause the arrogance of the proud to cease and will lay low the haughtiness of the terrible."

There was a blood moon tetrad back in 1949-1950 to commemorate Israel becoming a nation-state. There was a blood moon tetrad in 1967 when they won the six-day war. There was one in 2014 - 2015, which coincided with Passover and Sukkot.

Another amazing sign was the Revelation 12 sign that you can still use Stellarium Astronomy Software to look up; that happened on September 2017. "A great sign appeared in the sky, a woman clothed with the sun, with the moon under her feet, and on her head a crown of 12 stars. She was with child and wailed aloud in pain as she labored to give birth. She gave birth to a son, a male child, destined to rule all the nations with an iron rod." In the old testament, it clarifies that the 12 stars are the 12 tribes of Israel.

Event #35

When is Jesus' return likely to happen? God the Father says Jesus is His Son in whom He is well pleased. God's elegant solution from the foundation of the world is that God the Father would have His Son come down to the earth to solve the problem of sin and save us. The wages of sin are death, and Jesus took your sin, my sin, everyone's sin on the cross in the most excruciating way so that we could be redeemed back to Him and back to the Father.

This is the single biggest event ever done. I think God the Father would honor His Son by having the exceptional and terrible day of the Lord be on the same date He ascended. Jesus said, "I will return as I went". Historians can only produce a date range for when He was born based on clues of who was alive during the time of Jesus' birth; Herod, Pontus Pilot, and Gamaliel. So, Jesus was not born in zero AD.

Based on others alive between 6 BC to 3 BC. So, you would still end up with a range when the end of the tribulation might be.

If we were to take 2,000 years plus His age 33 = 2033. Let us look at the 3 BC number. 2033-3=2030 as the end of the tribulation. Now I am not a date setter, but as the Lord says, we can know the season we are in. 2030-7=2023. Anyway, 2023 or 2024 are likely times for the rapture. Given the latest finding for me, when Jesus says I will rise on the 3rd day, then the first 2 days are 2 thousand years, the beginning of the 3rd day would be the beginning of His rule and reign.

I know back in the 70s and at other times people have thought it is time for His return. But they did not understand that the last days' events must be global, thus happening to everyone everywhere, and with increasing intensity. Habakkuk 2:3-4 says, "For the vision is yet for an appointed time; but at the end, it will speak, and it will not lie: Though it tarries, wait for it; because it will surely come, it will not tarry. Behold the proud, his soul is not upright in him, but the just shall live by faith." This makes sense given several times that generations thought they were in it but were not yet.

This makes one ask the question; Why would the Lord tarry? He loves us all so much. He will save as many as He can until there are no more to be saved. Romans 11:25 "Lest you be wise in your sight, I do not want you to be unaware of this, my mystery brothers; a partial hardening has come upon Israel until the fullness of the Gentiles has come in (the Church will be full). I will not add to what the Bible says. The Bible is our rudder; it shows us what direction we should take. It would be impossible for anyone to come down to a day and hour. The Lord says "No one knows the day or hour" just to be clear. However, for Christians who may read this, here is 1 Thessalonians 5:4 "But ye, brethren, are not in darkness, that that day should overtake you as a thief. Ye are children of the light, and the children of the day; we are not of the night, nor the darkness. Therefore, let us not sleep as do others, but let us watch and be sober. 5:8 But let us who are of the day be sober, putting on the breastplate of faith and love; and for a helmet, the hope of salvation."

Event #36

Not to scare, but to share so that you can be prepared and find the Lord while it is day. I love you, whoever you may be, because God's love is so huge for you, and He gave me this same love, to love you with an intensity to write this for Him. There are other books I have considered writing in the past, but this one God poured out so that you could be saved; In order that you could experience a special relationship with God that is unique to you and Him.

Track the things written here for yourselves so you can know that God is going to complete everything in His word. You can look these up and see events even are happening after reading this, that you would turn to the Lord while there is still time.

On the World Economic Forum website, there is a page for what they call "The Great Reset." This is not a conspiracy theory, as they are now blatantly claiming what they are up to, and they think in their twisted way that they are the ones with the where-with-all to save all of us from global destruction because of climate change. They say they are taking the teachings of the Covid-19 crisis to improve the state of the world. The WEF is not a country, it is run by global elites like Klaus Schwab, the CEO of Pfizer Albert Bola, Microsoft, Elon Musk, and others. Do these elites represent you, or your best interests? They say they do, and that they have an imperative given their control of resources and knowledge to decide for each of us what is the best course of action and take it on our behalf. Wasn't there someone called Adolph Hitler who thought the same thing?

They call themselves global stakeholders. How corporate of them. If you have ever worked in a larger corporation, they use this "stakeholder" identification for the ones in the company who get to decide our course. Interesting, did you vote for them? Did you vote for any of their initiatives? To decide outside of our democracy what is right for me/us just doesn't fly. I'll stick with the Declaration of Independence of the United States that says I have the right to pursue life and happiness.

They state they will shape the recovery of national economies, the priorities of societies, the nature of business models, and the management of a global common. Why does this sound familiar? Ah, Adolf Hitler had such grand plans.

Vladimir Putin is fighting a war to have a bigger piece of the global pie that will be vetted out for countries that will fit in ten regions. Why ten? That is how many there will be when they split it all up, as stated in Revelation. China will do similarly with Taiwan, they have attended WEF meetings and know they also could be affected so they want an expansion of regions as well. They are powerful men who have been pushing for world dominance and it says about them: Revelation 17:12 "And the ten horns you saw are ten kings who have not yet received royal power, but they are to receive authority as kings for one hour, together with the beast."

Yes, the irony is that God will limit them to one hour of power. This reminds me of Psalm 2:2 "The kings of the earth set themselves and the rulers take counsel together against the Lord, and against His anointed (Jesus) saying: Let us break their bands asunder and cast away their cords from us. He that sits in the heavens shall laugh; the Lord shall have them in derision. Then shall He speak unto them in His wrath and vex them in His sore displeasure."

Be assured of one thing. God is not fooled, as He states, and He knows men's hearts, regardless of what they say or their deceiving actions.

Event #37

Matthew 24:12 "And because iniquity shall abound, the love of many shall wax cold, but he that shall endure unto the end, the same shall be saved. And this gospel of the kingdom shall be preached in all the world for a witness unto all the nations; and then shall the end come." 1 Thessalonians 5:3"For when they shall say, "Peace and Safety" then sudden destruction will come upon them, as travail upon a woman with child; and they shall not escape." Who was the apostle Paul talking about here? He means those who are asleep in their sins. Did you know that the words "Peace and Safety" are being used right now? By whom? The UN Security Council. They even have a statue known as "The Guardian for International Peace and Security," which is currently removed as it resembles "the beast" as described in Revelation; exact. Those interested can find it on the "Way Back" machine. Thank God for those who will preserve history of all things on the Internet.

In the Abraham Accords, "Peace and Safety" for the Middle East is called out. The Pope also echoed these words in his encyclical "Laudato Si" where he calls out all faiths to pursue fixing our planet for climate change. Let me be honest (always) and say that I am all for being good stewards of the earth. But not at the expense of individual freedoms as the Lord gives and as our country had for two hundred and forty-nine years. Ask yourself this: do you ever get the feeling lately that you are waiting for the other shoe to drop in your spirit?

Chapter 7
Future Events that are a "NOW" word.

Event #38

Don't be sad! Although this is the future, I want you to understand that we are right on the doorstep of tribulation, and in fact, it is a divine setup for it. Please don't wait until the tribulation has started to turn to Jesus. Do it now and get raptured with us who believe! I will not go into a huge dissertation on pre-trib, mid-trib, and post-trib. It doesn't affect those of us who are Christian except that a merciful God is not going to sludge His bride through hell on earth. He says that we are not appointed to wrath: 1 Thessalonians 5:9 "For God has not appointed us to suffer wrath, but to get salvation through our Lord Jesus Christ." All who accept the mark of the beast will be eternally damned. This is the truth, and I don't want anyone to discover this in the tribulation as if you accept Jesus, you will lose your head and be martyred for not accepting the mark. Do not make the new age mistake, the lie of the devil that hell doesn't exist. I once saw a man wearing a T-shirt that depicted Hell, and it said, "Hell is our party." You can be misguided now, but it is anything other than a party. It is torture by demons who can do this 24x7 if they want to. It is so hot you cannot stand it, but you have no choice. It is hard to breathe, and you smell sulfur all the time. Again, please watch Bill Weiss if you want the truth about hell as he had a brief visit there, and it is as it says in the Bible. Do not wait until you are there and can't do anything about it. Jesus said, "I am the way, the truth, and the life, anyone who believes in me, though he perishes yet shall he live!" Hell is real, heaven is real, believe someone who is on her 13th time reading through the Bible (me).

The Bible is unfolding as we speak. I was all done with this book except for some minor items to correct, and then an amazing revelation happened. from God. I was up late as I could not sleep, so I watched this man (Channel Generation2434, sorry I don't know your name) and he shared what he found on the UN website. The Secretary General had a report and this is the item of monumental interest "I urge Heads of State and governments to recommit to seven years of accelerated sustained and transformative action both nationally and internationally to deliver on the promise of SDG's."

What are SDGs you may ask? They are sustainable development goals. They sound harmless but they are what satan will use to deceive the world when we are gone. Here is the list:
1) No poverty
2) Zero hunger
3) Good health and well being
4) Quality education
5) Gender equality
6) Clean water and sanitation
7) Affordable and clean energy
8) Decent work and economic growth
9) Industry innovation and infrastructure
10) Reduced inequality
11) Sustainable cities and communities
12) Responsible consumption and production
13) Climate action
14) Life below water
15) Life on land
16) Peace, justice and strong institutions
17) Partnerships for the goals (yeah consider this corporate / multinationals)

So now let's turn to Daniel 9:27 that says "And he shall confirm (means the same thing as recommit or close enough) the covenant with many for one week." The "with many" would be many nations as this is the U.N. we are dealing with here. I thought about what Generation2434 was sharing here and it follows that there is pride before the Fall (this fall) and that Dr. Barry Awe has pinned down a good timeframe for the rapture, and that the fall at Shabbat would be a good time to start the tribulation.

Then I cried out to the Lord "Lord would you share with me something you have not shared with anyone else; PLEASE!" He answered me immediately with, "Go look up the Revelation 12 sign from 2017. The date." So I did and it was Sept. 23, 2017. then He let me know; count the years since the sign. I did and it is 6 years, and I realized what He was telling me. We thought the Revelation 12 sign was for us Christians and it is not. The sign was for Israel for the start of the tribulation. The tribulation is going to start sometime on September 23, 2023 making it exactly 6 years to the day. 6 stands for the antichrist and it makes this all the more clear.

We are told in the Bible that we won't know the day or the hour for the rapture, although I believe Dr. Barry is correct. But there is nowhere in the Bible that it says we can't know the date when the tribulation starts!

God is so good, that He has revealed it right now when all the watchmen are in concert together around these dates. God is good, and we fly before, and on September 23, 2023 tribulation begins when they "recommit / reconfirm" the plans of the evil one whom they serve. Generation2434 said we are on Rap-con One, but I believe we are at Rap-con 4.9999999.

Event #39

The rapture will be wonderful! Don't miss this experience! The Bible does not say "All who do the best works the Lord will save." No, rather it says those who believe in His Name will be saved. Romans 10 "For it is with your heart that you believe and are justified, and it is with your mouth that you confess and are saved." As the scripture says, "Anyone who trusts in Him will never be put to shame." For, "Everyone who calls on the name of the Lord will be saved." Yay! The Lord is going to separate the wheat from the chaff (you can't eat the chaff). This wind assisted process for separating the wheat from the chaff is called "winnowing" and the grains with almost no hull are called "naked."

Matthew 3:12 "His winnowing fork is in his hand, and He will clear His threshing floor, gathering His wheat into the barn and burning up the chaff with unquenchable fire."

Luke 17:34-36 "Then two men will be in the field, one will be taken and one will be left. Two women will be grinding at the mill; one will be taken and one will be left."

The Parable Of The Ten Virgins: Matthew 25 "At that time the kingdom of heaven will be like 10 virgins who took their lamps and went out to meet the bridegroom. Five of them were foolish and five were wise. The foolish ones took their lamps but did not take any oil with them. The wise ones, however, took oil in jars along with their lamps. The bridegroom was a long time in coming and they all became drowsy and fell asleep."

"At midnight, the cry rang out: "Here's the bridegroom! Come out to meet him!" Then all the virgins woke up and trimmed their lamps. The foolish ones said to the wise, "Give us your oil, our lamps are going out."

"No, " they replied, there may not be enough for both us and you. Instead, go to those who sell oil and buy some for yourselves." "But while they were on their way to buy oil, the bridegroom arrived. The virgins who were ready went in with him to the wedding banquet. And he shut the door."

"Later the others also came, "Lord, Lord; they said open the door for us!" But He said, "Truly I tell you; I don't know you." "Therefore, keep watch, because you don't know the day or the hour."

This story is about Jesus, who is the Bridegroom. The ten virgins are the church, and the oil is those who have an actual relationship and intimacy with the Lord and are keeping our oil and lamps ready for His return for us. There is no cheating on this.

Parable of the Wedding Feast: Matthew 22 "And again Jesus spoke to them saying "The kingdom of heaven may be compared to a king who gave a wedding feast for His Son and sent His servants to call those who were invited to the wedding feast, but they would not come. Again, He sent other servants saying, "Tell those who are invited, "See, I have prepared my dinner, my oxen and my fat calves have been slaughtered, and everything is ready. Come to the wedding feast." But they paid no attention and went off, one to his farm, another to his business, while the rest seized His servants, treated them shamefully, and killed them. The King was angry, and He sent His troops, destroyed those murderers, and burned their city.

Then He said to His servants, "The wedding feast is ready, but those invited were not worthy." Go therefore to the main roads and invite to the wedding feast as many as you find." And those servants went out onto the roads and gathered all whom they found, both bad and good. So, the wedding hall was filled with guests.

But when the King came in to look at the guests, He saw a man there who had no wedding garment. And He said to him, "Friend, how did you get in here without a wedding garment? And he was speechless. Then the King said to the attendants, "Bind him hand and foot and cast him into the outer darkness; In that place there will be weeping and gnashing of teeth. For many are called, but few are chosen."

I want you to understand friends, brothers, and sisters. When we receive salvation, we are made new, like the parable of the old wine in old wineskins and new wine in new wineskins. We are not who we are when we accept Christ. We are new creatures in new clothing that He gives us to wear. This is not to say we are completely perfect on the day we accept. But the Lord takes us from glory to glory as He uses a refiner's fire to change us from the inside out. This calls us to be obedient to what the Lord requires of us.

Event #40

So that you can be prepared like the "Canadian Prepper," I am going to share the first few apocalyptic events with the unsealing of God's scroll by Jesus. You see that these have already been prepped by God with some of these current events, such that tribulation could occur any day now.

1) The white horse seal gets broken. The rider who is the antichrist goes forth conquering and to conquer.
2) The red horse was given the power to take from the earth, and that they should kill one another, and he was given a great sword.
3) The black horse has a balance in his hand. The gist of this one is that there will be famine and that things will be so expensive that a day's wage will just buy you some bread.
4) The pale horse is greenish, and his name is Death, and hell is followed by him. Power was given unto them over 1/4 of the earth to kill with sword, hunger, and with death and with the beasts of the earth.

These fearsome horses have dominion over the whole earth for what they will do. You can see with the war in Ukraine, that we are close on the warring front. We are also very close, as there is food insecurity in every country. Billions are not eating enough each day. We can also know that the peace we used to take for granted is not present. It is palpable, like the loss of love that many are feeling now. Death, well if I chose to, I could see that every day on mainstream media. (I choose not to.) Now is the day of salvation, friends. There is no more time to waste. The Lord says that when He snatches us away, it will be "In the twinkling of an eye." Well, that is not enough time to make a commitment to Jesus at that point. Another passage of scripture that backs up Revelation is Isaiah 24, in which Dave Wilkerson has a fantastic sermon on the Internet.

"See, the Lord is going to lay waste on the earth and devastate it; He will ruin its face and scatter its inhabitants - it will be the same for priest as for people, for the master as for his servant, for the mistress as for her servant, for the seller as for buyer, for the borrower as for lender, for debtor as for creditor. The earth will be completely laid waste and plundered. The Lord has spoken this word. The earth dries up and withers, the world languishes and withers, the heavens languish with the earth. The earth is defiled by its people; they have disobeyed the laws, violated the statutes, and broken the everlasting covenant.

A blight befalls the land; Therefore, the earth's inhabitants are burned up, and the vine withers; all the merrymakers groan. The joyful timbrels are stilled, the noise of the revelers has stopped, and the joyful harp is silent. No longer do they drink wine with a song; the beer is bitter to its drinkers. The ruined city lies desolate; the entrance to every house is barred. In the streets, they cry out for wine; all joy turns to gloom, and all joyful sounds are banished from the earth. The city is left in ruins, its gate is battered to pieces.

So, will it be on the earth and amongst the nations, as when an olive tree is beaten, or as when gleanings are left after the grape harvest? They raise their voices; they shout for joy; from the west, they acclaim the Lord's majesty. Therefore, in the east give glory to the LORD; exalt the name of the Lord, the God of Israel, in the islands of the sea. From the ends of the earth, we hear singing; "Glory to the Righteous One." But I said, "I waste away, I waste away! Woe to me!

"The treacherous betray! With treachery, the treacherous betray!" "Terror and pit and snare await you, people of the earth. Whoever flees at the sound of terror will fall into a pit; whoever climbs out of the pit will be caught in a snare. The floodgates of the heavens are opened, and the foundations of the earth shake. The earth is broken up, the earth is split asunder, and the earth is convulsed. The earth reels like a drunkard, it sways like a hut in the wind; so heavy upon it is the guilt of its rebellion that it falls - never to rise again. On that day, the LORD will punish the powers in the heavens above (the devil and demons) and the kings on the earth below. They will be herded together like prisoners bound in a dungeon; they will be shut up in prison and punished after many days. The moon will be dismayed, the sun ashamed; for the Lord Almighty will reign on Mount Zion and in Jerusalem, and before its elders - with great glory."

I almost decided not to include this, because it is part of the intimacy that I have with the Lord. Have things always been happy being a Christian? Well resoundingly, yes, there is the joy of my salvation. However, if we truly walk with the Lord, we also suffer what He suffers. He is sad for those who will not take up His offer these days. His heart is for the lost, that they may be lost no more. He gives every Christian the outstanding opportunity to evangelize so that others can be close to Him! The amazing miracles I have witnessed Jesus do on the streets just blow my mind. It is the most wonderful way I could spend my life with Him.

He gave me a dream (this part I would not have shared) and I was in heaven. There was a most intense light coming from Jesus, who was sitting in a large chair in front of me. He was in a white robe. His face was obscured as I was only given sight to see His chest and below. He took my hands in His lap and asked me if I would experience nails in my hands. Immediately my spirit and mouth said YES! I saw this great thing He was doing for me as fantastic! Yes please, so He took these two nails (one for each hand) and He did my left hand first. It seemed way more real than here when I was awake. He explained the nail was much thinner, and He also said He was masking some of the pain for me. He used his hand to push it quickly through my left hand. It was very painful, but still, I knew how wonderful this was for Him to give me a new intimacy with Him. Then He did my right hand. I thanked Him and then woke up. I immediately looked at my hands as I just knew there would be marks. It was more real than real.

There were no marks, but that does not take away from this wonderful event He did for me. He is Saviour; he is Lord, and I cannot stress the closeness I feel after this happened and still right now. This might sound undesirable to a non-believer, however, of all the miracles He has done (around 60 big ones in my life). This means the most to me. That He shared with me His suffering on a much smaller scale that He lovingly scaled back so that I could endure it.

I know many Christian pastors who, if you share eschatological things with them, will start talking about fear and drumming up fear. They avoid everything to do with this topic, mostly. Because the Lord loves me and gave me this task to share with you, He has made none of this scary or frightening to me. Jesus is the Spirit of prophecy as it says in the Bible, and He shared about this time and what it would be. I guess if He can share it regardless of scoffers or mockers, then I can as well, since He instructed me to. And I have always the joy of my salvation and the peace from the Lord that surpasses all understanding.

Post Log

For the Christian who may read this. I want to share something that I know grieves the Holy Spirit about the prophetic. One thing I can guarantee, event 41 here is those who make money off prophecies as if they were given a word every day or every week. I know rapture is so close, I may not even be here to see the impact of this book. But I trust the Lord will reach who needs to be reached by it and He will do the saving. The Lord said there would be many false prophets in the last days who would say things He did not say to them. My caution is although you may think you heard Donald Trump would have a second term right after his first one and have gone to great lengths to carry this on by saying he is the legitimate president, well if he were we would see him with the president's press secretary answering questions for the media.

The extent that false prophets are going to paint a rosy picture that sells books and gets umpteen views on their YouTube videos and gives them popularity doesn't make the Lord happy. He is not a show that gets trotted out like a tarot reader. There are prophetic things the Lord has shared over my life, 56-ish, and for each one, what He told me came to pass. Some of them were hard. There were years when I didn't receive any word. I have internal scars from reactions I got from people I told things to which did come to pass. And I will tell you that if even one thing is false, then you are not a prophet and in the Old Testament, you would have been stoned.

God's standard is the same yesterday, today, tomorrow, and forever. If He has put you in this one of the five-fold ministries, then buckle up for a bumpy ride and repeat exactly verbatim what He says, and if you aren't sure, zip it up. There are things that I just shared with my sister, and they are things from 50 years ago, or more. He will tell you what to say, to whom, and when. If not, keep confidence in Him, and that is important. I only and ever want to please my Lord.

I can say with certainty that with the prophets, He had and has a designated time for them to share what was and is on His heart and His plans. He said that He would tell the prophets first.

Amos 3:7-8 "God does nothing on the earth unless He reveals His secrets to His servants, the prophets". I was reluctant to include this as false prophets I have seen trot this passage out a lot. The difference is for me, there is not any desire other than to fulfill the Lord's will, and to evangelize as He wills it!

I have heard many pastors say that the Bible is 1/3 eschatological when contending for having pastors that never share about future events, to encourage them to do so. In fact, the Lord is the Word (and the Word was God and dwelt among us). Further the Lord is the Spirit of prophecy, so He is 100% eschatological, even His first word in the Bible "Bersheet" has a meaning that conveys the Father sending His Son and a tent that we are in with His Son tabernacling. See C.J. Lovick for a full breakdown of the Hebrew for Bersheet".

Last, thank you, Lord, for sharing all of this with me. You are beyond my wildest expectations and whatever you share is most amazing. I will love you forever, and shortly sing your praises in heaven as we all say, Holy is the lamb who was slain; All power and glory and might and riches to our Lord Yeshua Hamashiak. Forever there will be holy holes in your hands and feet, badges of what you did for me and us. Thank you for sharing with me, and for our two-way conversations.

Bibliography

1) Time Magazine article on fires with pictures from space of California wildfires.
2) Googled where hailstorms are for 3 years.
3) Googled where floods are for 3 years.
4) Droughts https://www.drought.gov & UN on drought.
5) CNBC on climate change desertification.
6) Googled dried-up rivers to get the global list.
7) Publication by Yale Environment 360 on rising sea levels.
8) Locusts 930 square miles in Northern Kenya Newspaper.
9) The Temple Mount Association on Red Heifers.
10) High-speed train in the Jerusalem Post.
11) Lord Allenby Balfour Declaration.
12) Georgia Guide-stones & Yosef Abramowitz & the Pope.
13) 10 Climate Change Commandments https://www.weforum.org see the plan for 15-minute cities.
14) Abrahamic Family House in Abu Dhabi.
15) Chuck Missler on YouTube, website ChuckMissler.com or khouse.org
16) Elon Musk-"The everything app."
17) Executive Order #14067 allows for U.S. CBDC.
18) Robert Kiyosaki and Lynette Zang understand the global finance system.
19) William Casey CIA Director quote.
20) Klaus Schwab desires to be the global king, find him on Youtube also on Redacted.

21) Bill and Melinda Gates $205 million invested in Pharmaceutical Companies. WSJ.
22) Bill Gates farmland purchases AP Wire.
23) Whitney Webb "One Nation Under Blackmail" Vol I and Vol 11.
24) Thomas Horn's "Shadowland"
25) BLM in the Seattle Times and on King 5 News.
26) Zeitgeist the movie can be viewed on YouTube.
27) Dana Coverstone on YouTube.
28) Bill Weiss talks about seeing hell in his book "23 Minutes in Hell."
29) Mary K Baxter "A Divine Revelation of Hell."
30) British Antarctic Survey on moss - A debunking of carbon dating.
31) Stellarium Astronomy Software - 2017 Sept. 23 Revelation 12 sign. It showed this sign in the heavens on this date that exactly matched with where it said in scripture that these celestial bodies would be.
32) Canadian Prepper - Thank you, brother.
33) Dane Wigington www.geoengineeringwatch.org including specialists he has had in-depth discussions with – Alan Buckmann, Catherine Austine Fitts, Chrinstine Trame PHD and others.
34) C.J.Lovick awesome presentations explaining Bible prophecy.
35) Dr. Barry Awe, the most knowledgeable on the Bible about the feasts, and God's timing.

The Heavens

About the Author

My name is Mary Young and I live in Lynnwood, Washington, and have worked in missionary work for 6 years serving the homeless and co-working with the Holy Spirit. I have a husband David, a daughter Laryn, my sister Kathy, two dogs, and a cat. I love my bible study sisters and also my prayer warrior sisters in Christ. Years ago when I was a teen, I prayed for lasting friendships and the Lord gave me deep friendships that have spanned the test of time.

Shout out to Katherine Scherer, Judy Bell, Karen Law and my recent reconnect with Florence Woodbrook, a Christian who I knew from Community College.

Don't wait to give Jesus your "yes" as I know we don't have too much more time here. I can promise you this, my Jesus will never disappoint you, and He will love having a close walk with you. I can promise if you give your life to Him, He will give you more love and peace that can pass all understanding. He shares so much of Himself. He is faithful, gracious, merciful, righteous and just, besides being the creator of everything.

www.ingramcontent.com/pod-product-compliance
Lightning Source LLC
Chambersburg PA
CBHW070336120526
44590CB00017B/2902